Tropical Rainforests

230 SPECIES IN FULL COLOR

a Golden Field Guide from St. Martin's Press

by ALLEN M. YOUNG, Ph.D.

illustrated by JUDITH HUF

St. Martin's Press ❧ New York

FOREWORD

Tropical rainforests are vast treasurehouses of biological diversity, fragile living laboratories in which the processes of adaptation can be studied. But they are vanishing at an alarming rate. Scientists believe that their present-day destruction, clocked at a loss of about 50 acres a minute, is equal to the disaster that wiped out the dinosaurs some 65 million years ago.

Although over time most species have become extinct due to natural events, extinctions today are mostly human-induced, and it is unlikely that many new life forms will evolve to take the place of the ones that are gone. Therefore, we must all do whatever we can to ensure the survival of the remaining rainforests.

I am very grateful to various curatorial staff of the Milwaukee Public Museum for their expert assistance in providing information on individual species and for reviewing drafts of the manuscript. I also wish to thank Caroline Greenberg and Maury Solomon, former Golden Guides editors at Western Publishing Company, for the support and guidance they gave to this project. I am also very grateful to Bradley Wood, my editor at St. Martin's Press for seeing the book through final production.

I am extremely grateful to Judith Huf for the excellent illustrations she provided for this book. It was a great pleasure to work with her.

—A.M.Y.

CONTENTS

INTRODUCTION

WHAT ARE TROPICAL RAINFORESTS? The areas designated by scientists as tropical rainforests—once popularly known as jungles—all lie in the rather narrow belt around the equator known as the tropics, which is bounded on the north and south by the lines of latitude called the Tropic of Cancer and the Tropic of Capricorn. At one time a nearly unbroken band of lush vegetation, tropical rainforests today are widely separated and highly fragmented, mostly due to the encroachment of modern civilization.

Tropical rainforests are extremely ancient environments. They developed on land that had deep layers of highly weathered soil depleted of nutrients by continuous heavy rains. The challenge of living on these poor soils established them as highly efficient networks of creatures and processes. Tropical rainforests survived even the onslaught of the last ice age, some 2 million years ago, when huge glaciers blanketed much of the Earth. Today they are magnificent assemblages of life-forms that have evolved over many millions of years.

Tropical rainforests around the world are hot and humid places. Daytime temperatures throughout the year generally range from 70° to 85° Fahrenheit (F) but may climb into the 90s.

Not surprisingly, rainfall in tropical rainforests is very heavy all year long. Near the equator warm air, which can hold more moisture than cold air, rises and moves toward the poles. As this warm air rises, it cools and rains most of its moisture down on the ground below.

The abundant rainfall, high temperatures, and nearly enclosed spaces created by the "roof" of dense foliage in tropical rainforests all combine to produce very high levels of humidity. The plants also give off huge amounts of water through a process called transpiration. In fact, at least 50 percent of the rain falling on tropical rainforests is water

High moisture levels and year long warmth lead to lush and varied growth

Temperate Forest Soil:

Thick layer of leaf litter

Deep-rooted trees in deep rich topsoil

Rapid decomposition and re-uptake of nutrients leave little humus or topsoil

Many years of heavy rains leach minerals from soil

Shallow layer of leaf litter

Shallow roots in shallow layer of topsoil

The Tropical Rainforest Paradox: Despite luxuriant growth, soil is poor

that comes from the organisms themselves—the plants and even the animals living inside the rainforests!

Although tropical rainforests generally average about 60 inches of rain annually, some get several hundred inches of rain or more each year. The rugged rainforested Choco region of Colombia in South America is one of the rainiest places on Earth, receiving more than 300 inches—that's 25 feet!—of rain each year.

In spite of the luxuriant plant life everywhere in tropical rainforests (about 100,000 of the Earth's 250,000 identified flowering plant species are found there), a quick look reveals few signs of animal life. This is deceptive. Literally thousands of species of insects and other tiny creatures thrive within small areas. Although tropical rainforests occupy less than 10 percent of the Earth's exposed land surfaces, they contain close to 70 percent of all plant and animal species. In addition, many of the world's biggest, smallest, and most ecologically specialized creatures live in tropical rainforests.

Insects make up the largest slice of biological diversity found throughout the world. They represent more than 90 percent of all animal life. About 80 percent of all insect life is found in tropical rainforests.

Several million species of insects, of which only about a million have been named and described by scientists, thrive in tropical rainforests. Consider this: If you could weigh all the ants that inhabit Brazil's Amazonian rainforest, they would outweigh all vertebrates in the rainforest (frogs, lizards, snakes, birds, and mammals) by about 4 to 1!

Tropical rainforests can help us to understand the many types of complex relationships that form among different groups of living organisms. Numerous examples of the various ways in which rainforest species interact have been included in this book.

The luxuriant plant growth of the Tropical Rainforest

Tropical Rainforests are less than 10% of the earth's land area

But they support nearly 70% of all plant and animal species

NONTROPICAL RAINFORESTS Not all rainforests are tropical. Many forests to the north and south, as far from the equator as Norway and southeastern Alaska, have enough annual rainfall to qualify as rainforests. But their large variation in annual temperatures and cold winters prevents these forests from being regarded as tropical. Temperate rainforests support a much smaller variety of animal and plant life than tropical rainforests.

Subtropical rainforests, with plants and animals more closely resembling those in the tropical rainforests, can be found in such places as Hawaii and Puerto Rico. However, like the long-isolated island-country of Madagascar, these small island forests have experienced long periods of isolation, and thus their plant and animal life is different from that of mainland rainforests and usually not as diverse.

A **Cloud Forest** in Central America.

On the tops of mountains in Central America are the so-called cloud forests, which are often enshrouded in mist. Cloud-forest trees are much shorter than lowland tropical rainforest trees, and their branches are usually covered with dense carpets of mosses, lichens, and ferns. The plants and animals in these high-elevation forests are often more like those in temperate zones than those in the lowland tropics.

Some tropical forests have long dry seasons alternating with relatively short rainy or wet seasons. Unlike trees in tropical rainforests, many of the tree species in these "dry" tropical forests shed their leaves, and most of the important activities of plants and animals, such as feeding and re-producing, are shaped by the long dry seasons. Unfortunately, most of Central America's dry tropical forests have been destroyed by the spread of civilization.

WHERE ARE THE TROPICAL RAINFORESTS? As stated earlier, tropical rainforests are widely scattered across the Earth's equatorial belt, with each region home to a large number of unique, locally evolved ("endemic") plant and animal species. Thus the species found in African rainforests are very different from those found in South America.

Central and South Americas, Africa, Southeast Asia, Malaysia, Australia, and the Indo-Australian island chain all contain tropical rainforests. The tropical island-country of Madagascar, off the southeast coast of Africa, also has rainforests. The largest portion of intact tropical rainforest is found in South America, in the Amazonian regions of Ecuador, Peru, and Brazil.

More than half of the land of existing rainforests lies today in only three countries: Brazil, in South America, with 33 percent; Indonesia, in Southeast Asia, with 10 percent; and Zaire, in Africa, also with 10 percent. Smaller portions can be found in more than 50 countries around the globe.

The most biologically rich tropical rainforest, Amazonia in South America, supports at least 30,000 species of plants alone, compared to about 10,000 in all of North

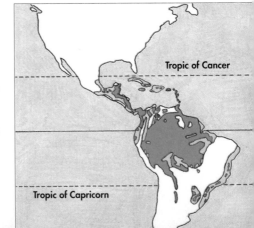

Key:

dark green =
present extent of
tropical rainforest

light green =
former extent of
tropical rainforest

Tropic of Cancer

Tropic of Capricorn

America. Tropical Africa, including the rainforests in the west, contains about 37,000 flowering plants, which is nine times more than that of all eastern North America. Amazonian rainforests contain one out of every five species of birds found on Earth, and the Amazonian river system contains at least eight times the number of fish species found in the entire Mississippi River system. Tropical rainforests in Latin America alone support at least a million species of plants and animals combined.

Madagascar, which is slightly smaller than the state of Texas, has 12,000 species of plants, compared to 743 in Texas. Between 80 and 90 percent of all the plants and animals in Madagascar are found nowhere else on Earth. What makes Madagascar's tropical rainforests particularly unique is 200 million years of isolation from the African continent (assuming it was once part of Africa) and the fact that all of its primates are monkeylike lemurs.

All the major rainforest regions of the world are discussed in this book. However, the greatest focus is on those in Central and South America, since these have the largest number of plant and animal species.

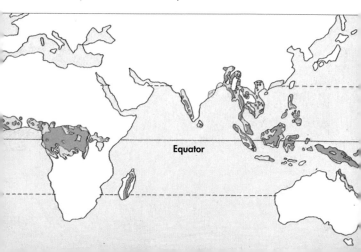

Equator

LAYERS OF A RAINFOREST A rainforest is not a single environment. Rather, it is a mosaic of environments, each part of which contains a unique assortment of living organisms.

Looked at from top to bottom, a tropical rainforest contains several distinct "layers." The uppermost of these is the rooflike canopy, where the leafy branches near the tops of trees stretch upward to catch the sunlight. The canopy is usually about 150 feet above ground level, though some individual trees may stick out as much as 50 feet above this.

The upper branches of the giant trees intertwine with their neighbors to form a dense latticework and support structure to which other plants can cling. Here, bathed in sunshine and amid lush vegetation, is where most of the animals in the rainforest live. The canopy is home to birds, monkeys, bats, tree frogs, snakes, and many insects (especially ants) and other arthropods.

Mats of rotting plant debris can become lodged in tree branches at different heights, providing homes for animals and fostering the growth of other plants. Tropical canopy trees are also festooned with epiphytes—plants growing on plants—and giant woody vines called lianas. The highest canopies in the world are found in the Indo-Malayan rainforests, which also support the world's richest diversity of gliding vertebrates.

Beneath the canopy are several layers of smaller trees that make up the understory, which extends from the forest floor to the lower levels of the canopy—a range of 50 to 80 feet. Because less sunlight finds its way here, fewer animals live in the understory than above it, though many move back and forth between the understory and canopy.

At the lowest level is the forest floor. Contrary to the impenetrable "jungles" of legend, the bottommost portion of the tropical rainforest—which is mostly in the shadows—is largely free of dense vegetation. Only 5 percent of the sunlight that falls upon the canopy reaches the forest floor.

Growing among the trunks of the great trees can be found decaying vegetation, seedlings, and various small plants. Few large animals inhabit the forest floor, most preferring the canopy and the understory, where they are less vulnerable to predators. The poison-dart frogs of Central and South America feed, mate, and lay their eggs on the forest floor but place their tadpoles in the canopy's water-filled bromeliads and tree holes.

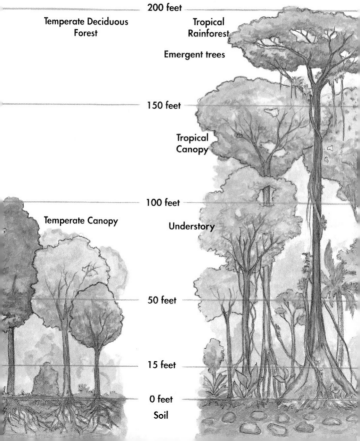

200 feet

Temperate Deciduous Forest

Tropical Rainforest

Emergent trees

150 feet

Tropical Canopy

100 feet

Temperate Canopy

Understory

50 feet

15 feet

0 feet

Soil

PHYSICAL FEATURES OF A RAINFOREST Most temperate forests have relatively few species of large trees but many individuals belonging to each. Most lowland tropical rainforests have fewer individuals but many more species. Rainforest trees of the same species may be spaced more than a mile apart! In temperate forests numerous members of the same tree species are often found clumped together.

Some rainforest trees, especially the giant trees of the canopy and emerging layers, have thick buttresses, or broad bases, which provide anchorage in shallow soil and help trees avoid the many clinging vines known as lianas. These buttresses are popular perching sites for birds such as vultures, whose solid wastes provide vital nutrients for the tree. Buttresses give the tropical rainforest a very distinctive appearance.

Roots in tropical rainforest trees generally spread out along the ground rather than penetrate deep into the

soil. To get around obstacles, some palms send out new roots, called stilt roots, farther away or in another direction, after which the lower trunk and older roots rot away.

Lianas often comprise about 25 percent of living matter in the rainforest. They can attain the thickness of a man's thigh and extend over 1,000 feet, binding themselves to trees with special hooks, glues, and tendrils. These long woody vines get nutrients from the forest floor but produce their dense foliage, flowers, and fruits in the canopy.

Mammoth, ropelike lianas can tie canopy trees together, adding structural stability to the rainforest. Lianas are also eaten by many rainforest animals. However, because lianas can slow down host-tree growth and eventually kill the tree, some trees produce smooth, flexible trunks and elongated leaves to discourage lianas from climbing up them.

Epiphytes, including mosses, lichens, ferns, orchids, bromeliads, and various parasitic plants such as mistletoes, also grow on the branches of tropical rainforest trees. Living mostly in the canopy, epiphytes are exposed to the sun and rain and are capable of absorbing water and nutrients directly from the air.

Some epiphytes have tough leaves coated with a wax-like substance that protects them from drying out under windy conditions. Many have showy flowers pollinated by animals, including insects, hummingbirds, and bats.

MICROCLIMATES The concept of microclimates provides an important key to understanding rainforest life. Some places in the rainforest are drenched in sunlight; others stay shaded most or all of the time. Within the generally wet and dense foliage are also many pockets of hot, dry air. Some places are exposed to wind; others are sheltered from it.

Tropical rainforests have open sections along rivers and streams. The direct sunlight causes temperatures in these areas to be much higher, and there is less humidity here than in the understory. Many animals make their homes on the edge of the forest along the rivers and streams.

A light gap, or opening in the canopy, can suddenly be

created when an old tree or a tree struck by lightning crashes to the ground. Soil on the forest floor is home to many unique kinds of ants and other tiny creatures. Beneath the leaf mulch—the dead and rotting leaves—on the forest floor, the ground is hard and claylike and is laced with strands of tiny roots woven together in a dense maze or tangle. When light gaps form, seeds that have long remained dormant in this litter respond by germinating and establishing new patches of vegetation.

All of these features of the rainforest environment plus some others result in the establishment of a multitude of different tiny climatic zones called microclimates. And within the individual microclimates, a large variety of organisms has evolved that has become specially adapted to them.

Forest Floor with Stinkhorn Fungus, Red-kneed tarantula—*Brachypelma smithi*, Millipede, and Hercules Beetle.

ENERGY AND THE FOOD CHAIN Most of the energy that powers life on Earth comes from the sun. Energy is distributed among the world of living organisms along food chains, which are made up of producers (plants) and consumers (animals). Plants produce and store the food, which contains energy from the sun, and insects and other animals eat the plants and assimilate their energy. Other animals then eat the animals that ate the plants.

In tropical rainforests food chains are very diverse and complex and include many different species of interacting plants and animals. Understanding the rich biological diversity of the tropics means, to a great extent, understanding food chains.

Food chains usually begin with photosynthesis. This is the process whereby plants capture the energy of sunlight and convert it, using carbon dioxide in the air and water, into carbon-based molecules that other organisms use for food. The vegetation produces energy-rich foods in the form of flowers, foliage, seed fruits, roots, stems, and trunks. These then become sources of energy for all other creatures on Earth. The plants also give off water and oxygen in the process.

Most rainforest leaves absorb rainwater directly, and many have long, pointed ends called drip tips that the rainwater rolls off to prevent mold and mildew. Bacteria, fungi, insects, and other small creatures help to recycle nutrients by quickly breaking down the decaying remains of plants and animals into forms easily absorbed by the roots of living plants. Little or no nutrients are left in the soil to be washed away with the rain.

The tropical rainforest captures and mobilizes a greater amount of energy through its vegetation than any other ecosystem on Earth. This huge reservoir of energy is the basis for the rich diversity of life that abounds there.

CHEMICAL WARFARE Animals that feed on plants are part of an intense biological tug-of-war, a struggle for existence that is constantly and dramatically played out among species in tropical rainforests. Living green plants represent a large, relatively immobile food supply for many animals, especially insects.

Because these herbivorous insects may kill or injure the plants, plants have evolved ingenious ways to defend themselves against the onslaught. Some plants have knifelike hairs and spines that impale or kill soft-bodied insects such as caterpillars. Other plants produce sticky resins that seal shut the insects' mouthparts. Many insects, however, have evolved counteradaptations to overcome plant defenses. Because tropical rainforests contain so many types of insects (of which 80 percent are plant eaters), the struggle between plants and animals is continually escalating.

By far the most impressive weaponry that some plants have evolved are the chemicals stored in their leaves, stems, and other tissues that make them poisonous or distasteful to eat. Interestingly such chemical deterrents in many instances have proven to be medically useful to people.

Sometimes closely related species of plants exhibit very different defenses against herbivores. For example, some species of Central American acacia trees in dry forests have swollen thorns that house colonies of certain species of pugnacious ants. These ants guard the trees by stinging any creatures that attempt to eat the plants, including other insects and browsing mammals. Acacia species with ant colonies produce tiny fruiting bodies on their leaves that provide food for these ants. Other species of acacia lack both the swollen thorns and the fruiting bodies but produce powerful chemical defenses that make up for the lack of insect allies.

Most species of rainforest insects feed on only one or at most a few kinds of plants, having evolved some adaptation that allows them to avoid that plant's chemical defenses.

(Upper left) **Derris**—*Derris elliptica*, Native peoples in Asia use the ground roots to stun fish, which are then harvested for eating. This vine is the source of the insecticide, rotenone.

(Upper right) **Passion Flower**—*Passiflora sp.*, caterpillars which feed on this vine become distasteful butterflies (page 62).

(Lower left) **Curare**—*Chondrodendron tomentosum*, Native peoples of tropical America use arrows tipped with poison obtained from this plant for hunting. This vine is the source of the drug Curare which is used as a muscle relaxant in surgery.

(Lower right) **Lycaenid Caterpillars**—*Eumaes mynas*, feeding on a poisonous Cycad become themselves poisonous.

21

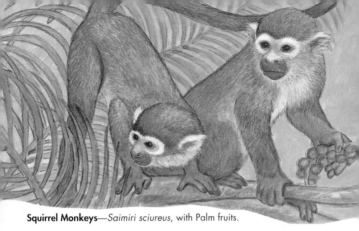

Squirrel Monkeys—*Saimiri sciureus*, with Palm fruits.

What repels one insect may actually attract other insects that have evolved a taste for that particular substance.

Insects aren't the only plant eaters. Monkeys, rodents, birds, and other animals also feed on foliage, fruits, seeds, and flowers. Along with herbivorous insects, these animals are able to extract and absorb nutrients and water from the plants—thereby incidentally providing a food base for carnivorous animals (meat eaters).

Rainforest monkeys often devour huge quantities of young leaves, seeds, fruits, and flowers from many different tree species. The movement of monkey troops through forests is largely determined by the availability of new growth on trees. Monkeys also eat insects and other prey.

Sloths in the New World tropics feed on the foliage of certain trees. They use the interlocking crowns of trees in the canopy to move from tree to tree with relative ease.

Rodents on the forest floor, such as agoutis, pacas, and certain mice, browse upon seeds and seedlings. The world's largest rodent, the Capybara, which grows up to four feet long, feeds on seeds in the Amazonian rainforest.

ANIMAL CAMOUFLAGE AND WARNING COLORATION

Camouflage, or crypsis, is a protective adaptation used by many kinds of animal prey. Cryptic insects have color patterns matching their background and exhibit various kinds of defensive behaviors. Katydids, for example, are green and brown and have leaf-shaped wings that look like real leaves. In some species the forewings have holes and notches that resemble the damage caused by insect feeding!

The caterpillars of many butterflies and moths match their background almost perfectly. Many kinds of rainforest butterflies, including Blue Morphos (see p. 60), rely on muted earth tones on the undersides of their wings to hide them from lizards on the forest floor. The upper sides of the wings of these same butterflies are typically covered with iridescent blue scales that produce a flashing blue pattern when the insects are in flight. When feeding on fruit on the forest floor, these butterflies hide from predators by holding their wings tightly shut above their bodies. Some species of rainforest walking sticks resemble twigs covered with mosses and lichens. Many frogs, toads, and lizards are also well camouflaged by their coloration and shape.

This insect, a rainforest **Walking Stick**, looks like the moss and lichens in which it lives.

Warning, or aposematic, coloration is displayed by some insects such as the famed *Heliconius* (Passion Flower) butterflies (see p. 62) and by other animals such as poison-dart frogs (see p. 89). The bodies of these animals often contain or exude poisons that make them bad-tasting or toxic to predators. Species that feed on poisonous plants often have warning coloration. They can absorb toxic chemicals from the plant and use them as defenses in their own bodies. Some rainforest spiders display warning coloration to advertise their venom and piercing bites to would-be attackers.

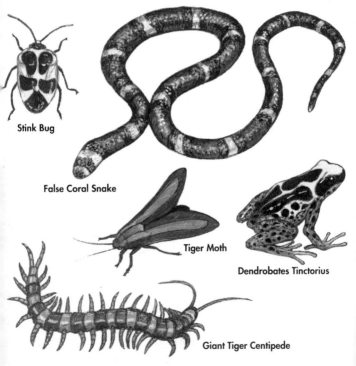

Stink Bug

False Coral Snake

Tiger Moth

Dendrobates Tinctorius

Giant Tiger Centipede

POLLINATION AND SEED DISPERSAL Not all is conflict in the world of rainforest plants and animals. Many plants take advantage of the presence of insects and other animal visitors. One example, that of acacia trees and the ants that live on them in dry forest, was given earlier. But most notable in terms of how rainforest plants and animals cooperate is the sexual process known as pollination. Tropical plants have evolved a number of methods for attracting pollinators, including brightly colored flowers, seductive fragrances, and mechanical trapping devices.

For the vast majority of tropical tree and liana (vine) species, there is no self-pollination. Pollen must somehow be carried from one flower to another, either between flowers on the same tree or—more commonly—between flowers on different individual trees of the same species. Due to the wide diversity of trees in the rainforest, the distance between individual trees of the same species is often great, and animals are the chief agents of pollen transport. The pollen itself is often sticky and rough-textured, allowing it to adhere easily to fur, feathers, or insect spines.

Flowering canopy and showy flowers attract pollinators.

Pollen is usually released when the plant's principal pollinators are most active. Some plants, for instance, open at night, while others open during the day. The pollen sacs of cacao flowers release their cargo at dawn, when tiny pollinating insects called midges are most likely to be present. In some plants the pollen is released explosively when sacs are broken free by visiting animals.

There are two major systems of pollination in tropical rainforests: long-distance and short-distance. Long distance pollinators include large bees and butterflies, sphingid moths, hummingbirds, other birds, and bats. The flowers of rainforest foliage pollinated by these animals are often large, showy, very fragrant, and produce large amounts of both pollen and nectar. Short-distance pollinators include flies, midges, small beetles, small moths, solitary and social wasps, and some butterfly species. The flowers they pollinate tend to be small and either white or cream-colored.

Bronzy Hermit Hummingbird— *Glaucis aenea,* at a Passion Flower.

Hawkmoth

Nymphalid Butterfly

Malachite Butterfly

Butterflies and moths are especially important flower pollinators. Butterflies generally visit large and showy flowers in open sunlight that are found along the edges of the rainforest, high in the canopy, or in light gaps.

Sphinx moths or hawkmoths visit flowers that store the nectar in long, narrow tubes. The scent of this nectar lures the moth, which then spreads the pollen to other flowers. Some nectarless flowers have evolved to look and smell similar to these blossoms. The moths are thus tricked into spreading the flower's pollen without the flower providing any reward for the moth.

One of the largest groups of vertebrate pollinators are bats, making up more than 50 percent of all mammal species in some tropical rainforests. Flowers pollinated by bats are typically either white or purplish, have a strong musty or sour odor, and are filled with sugar-rich nectar.

Seed dispersal is another important activity in the rainforest that interconnects plants and animals. Fruits and their seeds are highly nutritious and are often eaten by animals. Many different kinds are found in tropical rainforests; each kind attracts certain animals that feed on them and sometimes disperse the seeds without injuring them. Insects, parrots, toucans, hornbills, bats, monkeys, rodents, and even some fish disperse seeds. Ants are especially important dispersers of certain kinds of seeds. However, not all types of rainforest plants rely on animals to disperse their seeds.

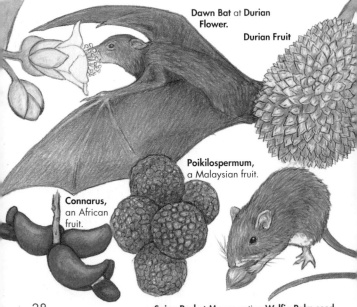

Dawn Bat at **Durian Flower.**

Durian Fruit

Poikilospermum, a Malaysian fruit.

Connarus, an African fruit.

Spiny Pocket Mouse eating **Welfia Palm seed.**

For example, the seeds of milkweed plants, among numerous others, are distributed by the wind.

The fruits of tropical trees are often brightly colored and have sweet-tasting pulp. The nutrients in fruits are designed to attract animals that will collect the fruits and carry them elsewhere to eat, discarding the seeds or passing them undigested far from the parent tree.

Birds and monkeys disperse the seeds of many trees, vines, and shrubs. The size, shape, and color of the fruit may determine which particular species will eat it and thus which seeds will be dispersed. However, birds and mammals generally avoid eating the fruits and seeds of toxic plants. As you can see, the interrelationships between living organisms in the rainforest are complex and can be fascinating to explore.

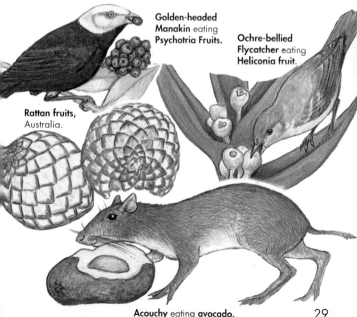

Golden-headed Manakin eating Psychotria Fruits.

Ochre-bellied Flycatcher eating Heliconia fruit.

Rattan fruits, Australia.

Acouchy eating avocado.

THE VALUE OF TROPICAL RAINFORESTS Perhaps the greatest value of tropical rainforests lies in the vast knowledge to be gained by studying them. Scientists often undertake grueling expeditions into these areas to learn about the plants, animals, and microbes there. Some focus on only one group of plants or animals; it might take weeks, months, or even years to determine, for example, how a certain kind of flower is pollinated. All of these field studies help cast light on the tapestry of life on Earth.

Rainforests are crucial in helping to balance gases and water in the Earth's atmosphere. They also aid in the formation of rain-laden clouds, which set global weather patterns.

Central and South American tropical rainforests are the wintering grounds for over 75 percent of all birds in North America. Many of these migrating birds spend up to seven months a year in tropical forests, feeding chiefly on insects to build up their fat reserves. Without the rainforests, many of these bird species would simply cease to exist.

Tropical rainforests are also important sources of certain wild plants used for cultivation of foods such as chocolate (from cacao) and bananas, and hardwoods such as mahogany. And many rainforest plants are now or could later prove to be important sources of medicine. However, the rapid destruction of the rainforests today is due in part by their commercial exploitation by outsiders. Thus, future efforts to obtain rainforest resources must be managed with greater wisdom, to avoid causing any further harm.

Female (left) and Male (right)
Scarlet Tanager.

HOW THIS BOOK IS ARRANGED In the five major sections that follow, species are generally grouped by standard scientific classification, or taxonomy. These correspond to the five major taxonomic classes found in the terrestrial rainforest environment—plants, insects and other arthropods, reptiles and amphibians, birds, and mammals. (Fish, which are not terrestrial, are excluded.) Since plants evolved first, these appear first in the book, and so on. Birds and mammals, it should be noted, evolved at about the same time.

The species chosen were meant to be a representative sampling of what can be found in various rainforest and related habitats. The more common species have usually been favored, though occasionally a particularly rare or fascinating or beautiful species was included.

Within each section, related organisms are placed near each other, and the entire sequence goes from approximately the most primitive (the groups that earlier branched off from a common species) to the most recently evolved. Where groups of species evolved at around the same time, the sequence will depend on other factors.

Where possible, single pages or spreads contain only species that belong to the same taxonomic order, although smaller groupings, such as taxonomic families, are used where deemed appropriate. Most reptiles, for example, belong to one of two different orders, so suborders are used instead. Some groups or single species have been placed in a catchall section at the end of the main section.

The major exception to this ordering scheme is the section on plants. Plants are a taxonomic kingdom rather than a class. Because the divisions within this kingdom bear little resemblance to the popular notion of plant types, we have chosen to group these species into more intuitive classifications. A more taxonomically correct grouping would scatter trees in various places throughout the section, which could be confusing.

PLANTS

PLANTS ARE THE ONLY ORGANISMS that acquire energy directly from the sun, through the process of photosynthesis. All other living things get their nourishment by consuming these energy-rich organisms, either directly or indirectly. Rainforest plants include the most beautiful and exotic organisms on Earth, from the fragrant and lovely orchids to the bizarre Strangler Fig. Many live in fascinating symbiotic relationships with insects, birds, bats, and other animals.

No one is quite sure how many different species of plants exist on Earth, though estimates range from less than 1 million to considerably more than 10 million. The majority of these species are found in tropical rainforests. Because of the huge number and types of rainforest foliage, many could not be discussed in this book. Fungi, mosses, lichens, and herbs, although they comprise a sizable portion of the plant biomass found in these complex ecosystems, have not been included.

Plants evolved at least several million years before animals. They are necessary for our very survival, not just because they provide food and oxygen for animals but because they recycle the carbon dioxide waste produced by animals back into oxygen.

For every acre of rainforest that is burned for farming space, uncountable numbers of individual plants and sometimes whole species are destroyed as though they had never existed. Many of these plants have never been classified by naturalists and may well have medicinal or other value. If the destruction of the rainforests continues at its current pace, thousands of plant species will become extinct within the next few decades.

Strangler Fig—*Ficus sp.* (far left) A seed left by a bird in a bark crevice of the host tree, sprouts and sends down a long root (center) The host tree is engulfed as the Strangler sends down more and more roots that fuse together (right) An empty cylinder of sturdy Strangler fig remains after the death of the host tree.

33

Ferns

Ferns may have first appeared on Earth more than 350 million years ago. Although seedless and flowerless, like seed plants they have roots, stems, and leaflike fronds plus vascular tissue to ferry liquid nutrients around the plant. Ferns are less common today than they were in the distant past, but there is still a great diversity of fern types, ranging from very tiny plants to treelike species towering more than 80 feet high. Ferns are found worldwide, but in the tropics most species are epiphytic (as mentioned earlier, meaning attached to huge tree trunks and branches) and prefer deep shade and dampness.

TREE FERNS range in height from 10 to 30 feet or more. They have treelike trunks and divided leaves that form their crowns. Usually found in small clearings in very moist areas, they are one of the first plants to appear in a light gap. The hard exteriors of the trunks of various species have scales, prickles, or spines. Since they reproduce by airborne spores rather than seeds, the distribution of ferns is uneven.

PENDANT FERNS, really fern-allies and not true ferns, are members of a large group of epiphytic plants including club mosses. They often bear stems and leaves that hang down toward the forest floor in the rainforests. Most striking are the club mosses, with their stems bearing leaves less than 1 inch long.

FILMY FERNS are small, delicate plants, although some can attain large size. They are named for their translucent, thinly textured leaves, which are characteristic of most species in this group.

Parasitic Plants

Rainforests are home to many kinds of parasitic plants, with Rafflesias being the most spectacular examples.

RAFFLESIAS have the largest flowers of all known plants, measuring up to 36 inches wide and weighing more than 20 pounds. The flowers rest on the ground and give off a strong odor, like rotting meat, to attract the kinds of flies that pollinate them. Rafflesias feed on the roots of their host plants. Several species are found in Indonesia, where they parasitize the roots of Possum-grape Plants.

MISTLETOES reach the height of their diversity in the rainforest. Small shrubs, treelets, or vinelike plants that can attach themselves to the branches of various trees, rainforest mistletoes often grow high up into the canopy and have their seeds scattered by birds. In the New World the tubular red flowers produced by most mistletoe species are pollinated by hummingbirds; in the Old World they are pollinated by flowerpeckers and sunbirds.

Vines

Vines are plants with long, flexible bodies that support themselves on other plants or structures, climbing or winding as they go, though a few vines—known as woody lianas—are quite huge and capable of supporting their own weight. The foliage, seeds, and fruits of vines are dined upon by many rainforest animals, some of whom scatter the vines' seeds. Young vines are vulnerable to insect browsing.

BENGAL CLOCK VINES are twining vines with broad, oval, hairy leaves up to 8 inches long and 3 inches across. The flowers are blue and yellow. The species is native to Asia. Because its natural pollinators are absent in the New World, this ornamental vine can survive here only by propagated cuttings.

MONSTERAS, found wild mostly in Central America, are noted for the variability of their leaves. The leaves of the young plant are less than 1 inch wide, round, and smooth-edged. The seedling contains no leaves at all until it begins to twine about a tree trunk. As the vine grows, the leaves become larger and longer—up to a foot in length—and form multiple fernlike lobes. The very largest leaves can be more than 3 feet long. At the top of the tree, the vine will reverse course and grow back down to the ground, its leaves becoming smaller again.

OX EYE VINES, found in Central and South Americas and also known as cowitch, are woody vines with hairs on their seed pods that can irritate or sting intruders. The leaves, which are pointed, can grow up to 7 inches in length, and the purple and yellow clustered flowers can have stalks more than 4 feet long.

Orchids and Bromeliads

Orchids, which are one of the largest and most widely distributed families of flowering plants, are found everywhere except in the Antarctic and the driest of deserts. The greatest diversity of orchids, however, occurs in the tropics, where there may be more than 25,000 different species.

Orchids blossom in an upside-down position relative to the stem. Some orchids—perhaps half the known species—are epiphytes. These, you may recall, grow on other plants, usually on the trunks and branches of trees, and are not rooted in the ground. Orchids depend on insects for pollination, and many have large and often very beautiful or bizzare-looking flowers.

The bromeliads form another important group of rainforest epiphytes. This order of plant is noted for the fact that its leaves form a kind of holding tank in which the plant stores water, enabling many species to live in very hot, exposed areas.

DANCING LADY ORCHIDS are epiphytic orchids with sword-shaped or sickle-shaped leaves about 2 inches long. The flowers are less than 1 inch across, with yellow and brown petals. This wide-ranging species is found from Mexico to Bolivia and Brazil.

VANILLA ORCHIDS are vines that grow up tree trunks, leaving their roots exposed to the air. The leaves are about 8 inches long, and 2 inches wide. The flowers have a strong fragrance and are greenish yellow. Found from Florida to South America, these orchids are the original source of the vanilla flavoring used in foods. The plant is grown commercially throughout the tropics.

TILLANDSIA BULBOSAS, like all bromeliads, are epiphytes. They hang suspended from tree branches. The leaves, roughly 6 inches in length, are twisted and rolled. The stalks are short and red, with up to eight flowers and spikes each. These plants are found from Mexico to northern Brazil and Ecuador.

(Upper right)
Stanhopea costaricense

(Middle left)
Sobralia rosea

(Middle right)
Telipogon sp.

(Lower left)
Masdevallia angulifera

(Lower right)
Dendrobium stratiotes

Other Plants

DIEFFENBACHIAS, and their close cousins, the **PHILODENDRONS,** are tall, conspicuous plants found in many New World rainforest areas. The broad, succulent leaves of these approximately 3-foot-tall understory and light-gap plants surround a white or light green sheath enclosing the male and female flowers. Beetles, which help pollinate the flowers, are drawn to them by their pleasant aroma. Various animals eat the good-tasting fruits but expel the largely inedible seeds. Dieffenbachias, also known as Dumb Cane Plants because they resemble sugar cane, often reproduce by using sucker shoots and form large, dense stands in the rainforest.

RATTLESNAKE PLANTS are named for their flowers, which resemble the "rattle" on the tip of a rattlesnake's tail. The pink or yellow flowers, sitting atop pairs of overlapping flat yellow disks, open in spring, summer, and fall. Their nectar attracts female orchid bees, among others, which "trip" the pollination mechanism as they try to reach the nectar. Birds disperse the bright blue seeds while feeding on the seed coatings. Found in Mexico, Central America, and northwestern South America, the plants range from 8 to 12 feet tall and usually grow in small clearings along the rainforest's borders.

LADY'S LIPS PLANTS are New World rainforest understory and light-gap shrubs often less than 5 feet tall. When in bloom, they have conspicuous red flowers. A pair of highly modified leaves form the bright red bract surrounding each cluster of small, yellowish, tubular flowers. Various species of butterflies and hummingbirds pollinate the flowers when feeding on the nectar. The sweet-tasting small blue fruits contain hard, oblong seeds. Birds feed on the fruits and swallow the seeds, which pass through the body unharmed and softened for sprouting new plants on the forest floor.

PIPERS are shrubs about 4 to 6 feet tall with spikelike hanging or upright flowers opposite the leaves on the stems. The tiny, whitish flowers are visited and presumably pollinated by various species of bees, flies, and beetles. Pipers are most commonly found in Old World rainforests, where there are about 500 species. The major dispersers of the small red berries, each of which contains a hard seed, are Carollia bats, which depend on piper fruits as the bulk of their diet. Bats may remove the seeds while flying or scatter them beneath night roosts many miles away. Hollow-stemmed pipers are used as homes by certain ants; these ants may protect the plants from being eaten by other insects. One species of piper is the source of pepper, a spice made by drying the fruits and then grinding them.

43

MILKWEED PLANTS are named for the milky latex usually stored in their stems and leaves. New World milkweeds are small, weedy plants with thin, upright stems. Slender, lance-shaped leaves grow along the full length of these stems. The yellow and reddish orange flowers that bloom throughout the year attract aphids and butterflies, which suck the sap from the stems and leaves.

BIRD-OF-PARADISE PLANTS, also called Heliconias, are 6 to 8 feet tall, with broad, erect leaves and red or orange upright or hanging bracts. Hummingbirds, which often visit the showy flowers in the morning hours, pollinate these South and Central American plants. The young, rolled-up leaves of Heliconias are home to various rainforest animals, including insect larvae, protozoans, frogs, and snakes, all dwelling in pools of collected rainwater, and nocturnal crickets and katydids. Hispine beetles feed on the soft tissues of the rolled leaves, leaving behind a line of evenly spaced holes once the leaf unfurls and the beetles are gone.

Trees

Trees are tall plants with upright woody stems, usually only one stem per tree. They are commonly grouped into one of two categories—evergreen or deciduous, depending on whether they shed their leaves in fall or winter (deciduous) or retain them throughout the year (evergreen). In tropical rainforests most trees are evergreen, if only because there is little seasonal temperature variation.

Trees are the most obvious species in any rainforest, towering above all other forms of vegetation and providing homes for a wide variety of animals and other plant species. Of the 70,000 or so species of trees that occur worldwide, about 53,000 are found in rainforests.

KAPOK TREES can be found in rainforests all around the world, including those in Ecuador, Brazil, Central America, India, Java, and West Africa. They have large roots that rise above the ground to form big buttresses. These buttresses help support the Kapok's huge trunk, which can be up to 100 feet tall and 10 feet in diameter. The trunk and branches are gray and spiny. Each leaf has from five to eight leaflets, and the white flowers have 4-inch-long fruiting bodies on them with thick skins. Fruit pods of the Kapok contain lightweight, water-resistant fibers called kapok, or silk cotton, which is used as a filling for life jackets, pillows, and upholstery and for insulating walls.

CORTES TREES produce masses of yellow flowers that bloom each year simultaneously on all the trees in an area. The flowers last for one week only. Found from northwestern South America through Mexico, these huge trees have grooved gray bark and large trunks that measure 10 feet around, and may grow to heights of more than 200 feet. Their leaves are composed of four to five big leaflets. The fruit is long and thin and produces "winged" seeds easily carried by the wind. Cortes timber is one of the hardest, strongest, and densest woods in the world. Mature trees are heavily harvested for furniture and other products.

PARA RUBBER TREES are native to the Amazon River valley in Brazil but have been exported to plantations in Sri Lanka, tropical Malaysia, and Indonesia, among others. The principal source of latex, a milky substance used to produce rubber, Para Rubber trees attain a height of 60 feet and have light gray bark, long and slender three-part leaves on long stalks, clusters of small flowers (no petals), and tiny capsules of fruit. The latex is collected by cutting a slit in the bark and "bleeding" the tree. Several other Amazonian rainforest trees also produce latex but are not exploited commercially for making rubber.

LIPSTICK TREES have spiny red fruit capsules, $\frac{1}{2}$ inch to 2 inches wide. Large, bushy trees reaching over 30 feet tall, Lipstick Trees are native to tropical America but have been cultivated elsewhere. The plant has large, heart-shaped leaves and 3-inch pink flowers that open before dawn and are visited by bees that gather the pollen. By afternoon the petals wilt and drop off. Pugnacious ants dining on nectar at the flower stems and base chase away other foraging insects. A fabric dye called annatto, which is made from the Lipstick Tree's fruit's juice, has been used to decorate the body since pre-Columbian times and to dye butter or cheese yellow or orange.

GAVILAN TREES are tall evergreens that are found, among other places, in southern Central America and northern South America. They reach a maximum height of 130 feet. Their leaves are similar to palm fronds, with many $\frac{1}{2}$-inch-long thin leaflets arranged along arching stalks. The flowering spikes, about 6 inches in length, have purple coverings. One spike holds about 200 flowers. White bark covers the tree's dark red trunk. Unlike most rainforest trees, Gavilans are often found in large clumps because their seeds are very poisonous and thus animals leave them alone wherever they drop, usually under the parent tree.

47

MONKEY POT TREES are very tall (over 150 feet high) and are found from southern Central America to South America. Vertical ridges mark the tree's dark brown bark. The single leaves are long and thin, and all of them drop off before the plant flowers. Pale blue and white flowers develop into the distinctive fruits resembling large, knobby coconuts. Almost a foot in diameter, the fruit has a 1-inch-thick wall, with a rounded cap measuring about 4 inches across. This breakaway "door" falls off when the seeds are ripe, allowing bats to remove them for food. The trees are named for this opening, which is said to be large enough for a monkey's hand to fit inside but too small to allow its clenched paw to remove the seeds.

MAHOGANY TREES are used to produce a wood that cabinetmakers have prized for more than four centuries. A few different species of tropical hardwoods share the name "mahogany." The first to bear it were trees found in Mexico, central South America, and some Caribbean islands. (Trees in African rainforests that produce similar wood are referred to as African mahogany.) Tall evergreen trees that can reach heights of over 100 feet and diameters of 20 feet at the base, mahoganies have large spreading crowns; compound leaves with four to six small, shiny, pointed leaflets; and distinctive woody fruits. The fruits, bulb-shaped and about 6 inches long, split open at the base to release their seeds. The tiny flowers are whitish or pale yellow-green. Since the trees are very difficult to cultivate, overcutting is threatening the survival of native populations.

WILD NUTMEG TREES are the source of two popular spices: nutmeg and mace. These evergreen trees, which reach heights of about 60 feet, are found in many tropical rainforests. But cultivated nutmeg is originally from the Molucca Islands of Indonesia and several New World rainforests. The fragrant oval leaves of Wild Nutmeg trees are dark green on top and a lighter color underneath; the tiny flowers range in color from yellow to green. The round yellow-orange fruit, about the size of a peach, has one almond-sized seed surrounded by a red meshlike coat called an aril. The seed is ground for nutmeg and the aril is dried to produce mace. Large Central American birds, such as toucans, are attracted to the fruit by its aril, which they eat, dropping the hard seed to the forest floor.

SURÁ TREES are found from Central America to the Amazon Basin and are a valuable source of timber. They derive their name from the Latin words meaning "oblong end," which refers to how the leaves are grouped together at the ends of the branches. Reaching heights of 150 feet, these trees have light brown bark and bear small yellow and green flowers in the winter months of December or January.

49

CYCAD TREES, occurring in both the Old and the New World tropics, look a lot like palm trees with their tall, columnar trunks and large crowns of dark, long, fernlike evergreen leaves that fan out in a circle around the flowers. Heights can range from about 3 to 6 feet. The American genus is found from the southern U.S. border to much of South America. Cycads are living fossils of one of the oldest-known plant families still in existence, dating back millions of years. Separate plants carry the male and female flowers. The male plants produce compact cones from which stingless bees and other small insects gather pollen; the female plant carries a larger, rounder cone with scarlet seeds. The leaves and cones of cycads contain powerful poisons, but a few insects, such as the caterpillars of certain hairstreak butterflies, eat the leaves. The roots are boiled and eaten by some Indians.

LAUREL TREES are found in Mexico, Central America, and parts of South America. (The name "laurel" applies to many tree species, not all tropical, including some trees found in the United States.) The swollen nodes found at branching points in the rainforest wood are an important identifying trait of the tropical species. These nodes are frequently colonized by Azteca ants. The trees are about 100 feet tall, with gray bark and rough-textured evergreen leaves that are white on their undersides. The tropical laurel bears a profusion of scented white flowers early in the year. The light-colored wood is used in making furniture.

CECROPIA TREES are evergreens native to northern South America and Central America. About 50 feet tall and 18 inches in diameter, they have hollow trunks and branches that are used by some tribes as musical instruments. For this reason, they are sometimes referred to as Trumpet Trees or Trumpetwood. The leaves are broad and multilobed, with a soft, textured, green-gray top and a bright white underside. When turned over, the leaves can resemble white flowers. Certain species of Azteca ants thrive as large colonies inside the hollow trunks and feed upon droplets of food produced by the plant at the base of each leaf. These ants have powerful jaws that are used to prune away any young vines found growing on the trunk of the tree.

RUBBER TREES are familiar to us mostly as houseplants. Members of the mulberry family, they were named for the latex that seeps out when the bark is cut, though they are less useful for producing rubber than the Para Rubber Tree (see p. 46). In the tropics, rubber trees can reach heights of 100 feet and have large, spreading crowns. The oval leaves, which have a glossy surface and a thick, leathery texture, grow close to the stem and may be a foot long. The edible fruit is a yellow-green fig about a half-inch across. Native to Nepal and Burma, rubber trees, which are evergreens, are pollinated by a complex mechanism involving gall wasps, which live out their entire lives inside the flowers.

WELFIA PALM TREES are found in southern Central America. They need a lot of light and heavy rain to grow and so tend to thrive in light gaps. The trees range in height from 25 to 65 feet, with dense crowns of heavy leaves. The flowers are arranged along a multibranched stalk. The white male flowers bloom first and last only about a day, opening in successive clumps. Then, all at once, the similar-looking female flowers bloom; these last for several days. The small, elliptical-shaped fruit is less than 2 inches long. It grows just below the crown of leaves covering the stalk and falls to the ground when ripe. Various species of these palms (but not all) yield useful oils and edible nuts. Many other rainforest palms have their nuts and seeds dispersed by rodents or other vertebrates.

INSECTS AND OTHER ARTHROPODS

INSECTS MAKE UP THE LARGEST ORDER of animals in the world, both in terms of sheer numbers and the number of different species. Not surprisingly, there are more species of insects in tropical rainforests than anywhere else. More than 800,000 insect species have been identified worldwide, but these are probably less than half the number of species that actually exist. The rainforest is very likely home to the vast majority of unidentified species. The diversity of plants, reptiles, birds, and mammals in the rainforest is astonishing, but the diversity of insects is almost beyond belief.

Insects belong to the phylum of animals known as arthropods, all the members of which have hardened shells or exoskeletons surrounding segmented bodies. Insects are distinguished from other arthropods by having only three pairs of legs, arranged in equal numbers along the front part of both sides of the body.

The great variety of insect and other arthropod life is presently threatened by the continuing destruction of the rainforests. Thousands of species are thought to have become extinct in just the last decade, most before they could be identified or cataloged by entomologists.

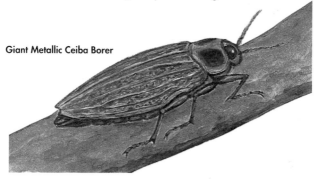

Giant Metallic Ceiba Borer

Grasshoppers

Grasshoppers, including locusts, are jumping insects. Though the young (nymphs) are wingless, most develop wings as they grow. To attract females, male grasshoppers—like their relatives, the crickets—make chirping noises and other sounds by rapidly rubbing their forewings together. Most grasshoppers feed on foliage or seeds. Rainforest species are most active at night and can fall prey to predators such as lizards, frogs, bats, and rodents.

GREEN-AND-GOLD GRASSHOPPERS, at about an inch long, are found in the Neotropics, mostly in rainforest light gaps. Wingless, they are green with golden heads, black stripes behind the eyes, and two long, white-tipped antennae. The prothorax (front of the body) and sex organs are also gold-colored. These grasshoppers engage in an unusual mating ritual. The male drums on plant leaves and the female replies in kind.

Green-and-gold grasshopper

Giant Red-winged grasshopper

GIANT RED-WINGED GRASSHOPPERS, from Central and South America, are so big they can look like birds. The female of this rather rare species is about 6 inches long and has a 10-inch wingspan. (The male, which is smaller, is still large for a locust.) The body has dark green and yellow markings and the hind wings, blue spots. The young are yellow with reddish brown tiger-stripe markings. These grasshoppers eat many kinds of shrubs and trees, including some that have powerful defensive chemicals in their foliage.

BUSH KATYDIDS, belonging to the genus *Orophus*, are familiar grasshoppers found in Central and South America. These 2-inch-long leaflike insects are usually greenish yellow or yellowish brown in color but may also be pink. Males produce their calls by rubbing their two forewings together when not in flight. Bush katydids live chiefly in the rainforest understory, where the brown forms closely match the color of dead leaves and the green forms, living leaves. Rainforests are home to many different katydid species, virtually all of which are active at night. Some feed on seeds, even though most species will devour vegetation. The seed-eating species have large, powerful jaws, capable of slicing through the tough seed coats many rainforest plants have.

Bush Katydid

Bush katydid

Brown False-leaf Katydid

Leaf Katydid

Yellow phase Bush Katydid

55

Cicadas

Cicadas are found worldwide but (like most other insects) reach their greatest diversity in the tropics. Costa Rica alone has about 30 species. Cicada larvae, or nymphs, burrow into the ground, where they suck on the sap of tree roots, emerging as winged adults only the lost few months of their lives. Male cicadas have a distinctive call, or song, and often sing together in trees, presumably to attract females. Cicada relatives include lantern flies and smaller insects such as leafhoppers, treehoppers, and aphids.

SUNDOWN CICADAS, about 1½ inches long, are often found on tree trunks, where their brownish color acts as a camouflage. The name comes from the insects' tendency to "sing" at sunrise and sunset. Its call is powerful and rather shrill. Mature nymphs of this species emerge from the ground in great numbers near tall legume trees, which are probably the food plants for the nymphs. The discarded, outgrown skins of cicadas can be found hanging from leaves nearly any time of the year.

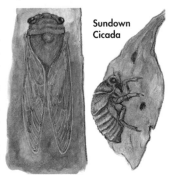

Sundown Cicada

LANTERN FLIES are found in Central and South America. Their grayish front wings and yellowish brown hind wings have prominent eye spots that blend in with the bark of Guapinol Trees and may frighten away some predators. When molested they release a skunklike odor. Lantern flies have 5-inch wingspans and large, odd-shaped heads from which they get their various nicknames, such as Alligator Head and Peanut Head. Their long proboscises can penetrate thick bark, allowing them to feed on plant sap.

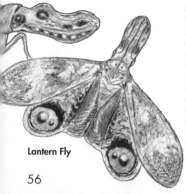

Lantern Fly

Beetles

Beetles are the most common of all insects. In fact, they are the most common animals on Earth, comprising more than one-fourth of all known animal species. The front wings of most beetles form a hard, protective sheath over the body, though a few species have no wings at all. The largest beetles grow to more than 6 inches in length. Although some beetles are carnivorous or scavengers, most are herbivorous.

DUNG BEETLES are members of the scarab family and were important symbols in ancient Egyptian art. Jet black in color and with a rounded shape, they are nocturnal by nature and grow to lengths of about $1\frac{1}{2}$ inches. They eat mostly animal droppings and lay their eggs inside dung piles, which the larvae later eat.

Dung Beetle

GOLDEN SCARAB BEETLES are less than 1 inch long. The flashy adults feed on the leaves of grapes and other vines in the rainforest. The fat white grubs feed on the roots of various plants.

Golden scarab beetle

HARLEQUIN BEETLES grow to about $1\frac{1}{2}$ to 3 inches in length and are brightly colored, with black, yellow, and red patterns that give them their name. Their antennae are several inches in length, and the front legs of the male are often longer than the body. These beetles are found in Central and South America, mostly from June to November.

Harlequin Beetle

RHINOCEROS BEETLES are named for the curved, hornlike projection that extends from the head of the male. This structure bears a striking resemblance to a rhinoceros horn. Males use their horns when fighting with other males over food or mates. Rhinoceros beetles grow to lengths of 2 to 3 inches and are dark brown in color. They are found in forests from Central America to the northern portions of South America and lay their eggs in rotting logs.

Rhinoceros Beetle

Rain-Tree Bruchid

RAIN-TREE BRUCHIDS belong to the Bruchidae, a family of seed-eating beetles that lay their eggs on seed pods and, after hatching their larvae, feed on the seeds. Some species can eat the entire seed crop of a stand of trees. The adult is about $\frac{1}{5}$ of an inch long and beige in color. Rain-tree Bruchids are found in Central America and the northern portions of South America.

Butterflies and Moths

Butterflies and moths are important rainforest herbivores. Moths are far more abundant than butterflies and usually fly at night. But like most butterflies, some tropical species are active during the day.

The largest butterflies and moths have wingspans of 12 inches or more. Some brightly colored species are very unpleasant to eat. Predators usually avoid them. The caterpillars of these insects often acquire their taste by feeding on plants containing defensive poisons. They are able to store these toxic chemicals without harm to themselves. The colors and patterns of toxic species are often copied by better-tasting species called mimics, who fool predators and thus gain themselves some measure of protection.

TAILED BIRDWING BUTTERFLIES, which include the spectacular New Guinea species with its 6-inch wingspan, are gaudily colored and taste very bad. They usually fly in the treetops but will also search for food near the forest floor. The females have grayish forewings and are larger and drabber than the males. They lay ovoid, yellowish eggs on poisonous vines called Aristolochias, and their caterpillars dine on the leaves for weeks. The adult butterflies sip nectar from the often reddish, showy flowers of various trees and vines.

Queen
Alexandra
Birdwing

Paradise
Birdwing

Rajah Brooke's Birdwing

59

Morpho peleides

M. amathonte

M. peleides

BLUE MORPHOS are among the most brilliantly colored butterflies. Most species are large and have bright blue, mirrorlike, iridescent scales on their wings. Found in South and Central America as well as the West Indies, *Morpho peleides* has a wingspan of about 5 inches. The wing's underside has earthtone markings and eyespots that may scare off predators such as lizards, which may mistake the insert for a larger animal as it feeds on the rotting fruits and fungi resting on the sun-streaked forest floor. *Peleides* caterpillars and some other species of *Morpho* feed on the foliage of rainforest legume trees and vines.

M. peleides life cycle with egg

PHARMACOLOGICAL SWALLOW-TAIL BUTTERFLIES, including the *Parides* and *Battus* genera of Central and South Americas, are colorful and toxic, like the Tailed Birdwings (see p. 59). The velvety purple and white tubercle-studded *Parides* caterpillars feed on highly poisonous vines. Some species from these genera have black wings with vivid red and yellow splotches and other markings; the males may also have bright green or blue-green markings. A strip of dense white scented hair along the inner edges of the male's hind wings attracts females. Males will often "patrol" rainforest clearings in pursuit of females. Several other species of butterflies, plus a day-flying moth from the genus *Dysschema*, mimic the highly distasteful *Parides*.

Parides childrenae adult

A mimic

Battus polydamas adult

Haeteera macleannania

Parides sp.

CLEARWING SATYRS, made up of species from both the *Cithaerias* and *Haetera* genera, are widespread though little-known butterflies found near the forest floor in Central and South America. Most *Cithaerias* have a wingspan of about $2\frac{1}{2}$ inches and a tinge of red, blue, or yellow on the hind wings; larger in size, the *Haetera* species has two eyespots on the hind wings. The wings in both these groups are nearly transparent, making the butterflies hard to see as they fly just above the ground, feeding on fallen and rotting fruits.

Cithaerias esmeralda

Cithaerias sp.

61

PASSION FLOWER BUTTERFLIES are chiefly from the genus *Heliconius,* a diverse group of New World rainforest insects. Along with the ithomiines (see p. 63), they are easily recognized by the oblong shape of their fore-wings. Passion Flower butterflies have wingspans of up to 3½ inches, have excellent vision, and can remember visual landmarks in their foliage-rich habitats. They prefer to lay their eggs on passion flower vine tendrils, safely hidden from marauding ants and other such predators, though razor-sharp hairs on these vines can impale and kill the newly hatched caterpillars. Adults collect pollen grains from the orange flowers of wild cucumber vines growing in light gaps. The pollen is a rich food that increases the females' egg production. Most species are unpalatable.

Passion Flower Butterflies

OWL BUTTERFLIES, which belong to the genus *Caligo,* consist of several large, similar-looking, widespread species from Central and South America. They take their common name from the large eyespots on the underside of their forewings, which resemble the eyes of an owl and may frighten away birds and other predators. Owl butterflies, which have 6-inch wingspans, fly at dusk and feed on the juices of rotting fruits. Males have scent patches on the abdomen that are used to attract mates, and eggs are placed on bird-of-paradise, banana, wild ginger, palm, and other monocot plants.

Owl Butterfly

BLUE, COPPER, AND HAIRSTREAK BUTTERFLIES make up a large group of relatively small but widespread butterflies in the family Lycaenidae. The caterpillars of some species are protected by ants that feed off nectar or honeydew exuded by special glands ___ _aterpillar. The cater-p___ _e species in a related __ _the metalmarks attract _s by "singing" to them, _al comblike structures on _s. Although most of the _rs of both groups feed on _some are carnivorous and _live in ant nests.

Metalmark Butterfly

Ithomiine Butterflies

ITHOMIINE BUTTERFLIES have a unique, fluttery flight and take deep wing strokes. With their diverse wing colors and patterns, species may mimic each other, heliconiines, or other groups. Found in Central and South America, the butterflies in this family have wingspans of 2 to 3 inches and clear, translucent amber or tiger-striped wings. Their forewings are shaped like the heliconiines, though ithomiines are more closely related to milkweed butterflies (see p. 64). Their chrysalises may be a silver or gold color, with the caterpillars feeding on members of the tobacco-tomato-eggplant family. Males have special hairlike scales on their hind wings that are displayed in courtship. They collect certain chemicals from plants from which they make a scent to attract females. These same substances, passed to the female during mating, may give her protection from predators.

63

MILKWEED BUTTERFLIES are a widely distributed group of rainforest insects with wingspans of 3 to 4 inches. Named for milkweed plants, which are the only food their caterpillars will eat, two widespread, familiar species of this group, found in both temperate and tropical areas, are the Monarch and Queen Butterflies. Male milkweed butterflies have special patches on their hind wings or hairs inside their abdomen to produce a scent used in courtship. Adults feed on nectar from a wide variety of flowers found mostly in light gaps or along the rainforest's borders. Because the milkweed plants the caterpillars eat are poisonous, the adult butterflies are mimicked by some other species, including moths.

Tropic Queen

Monarch

D. chrysippus

Monarch caterpillar, pupa, and adult female laying eggs on milkweed.

Urania Moth, Adult and larva

GREEN URANIA MOTHS have luminous green stripes on their black wings. Active in daytime, their wings are shaped like those of swallowtail butterflies. These large Central and South American moths can fly up to 25 miles an hour. Several times a year huge flocks of Green Uranias migrate over long distances in their search for the food plants of their caterpillars, certain toxic rainforest vines or lianas such as *Omphalea*, on which they lay their eggs.

64

WILD SILK MOTHS, with wingspans of up to 10 inches, have splendid color designs on their wings. Their huge green caterpillars, usually banded with various colors, graze upon a broad range of forest trees and vines. Some New World species have very long extensions on their hind wings, earning them the nickname of swallowtail moths. Those from more seasonal regions may move to rainforests to wait out the dry season and so depend on large expanses of habitat to survive, not just confined patches of forest.

Wild Silk Moths

Giant Sphinx Moth

SPHINX MOTHS, with their long, narrow wings and 2- to 6-inch wingspans, mimic hummingbirds and feed at tubular-shaped flowers. The Giant Sphinx Moth (*Cocytius antaeus*) of Central America has a tongue, or proboscis, almost 11 inches long! Because food resources are often sparsely scattered about, the moths must patrol large expanses of forest habitat to find enough nectar and caterpillar food vines. Being lavgely nocturnal, they often fall prey to bats searching for food.

Ants

Ants are social insects. There are more than 4,500 species worldwide, all of which live in large colonies, with a division of labor between the various "castes" of ant. Each colony is started by a pregnant female, who becomes the colony's queen. Ants reach their greatest diversity in the tropics, particularly in South and Central Americas, where the smallest and the largest ant species in the world are found. Rainforest ants nest in an extraordinary number of different environments and form many different kinds of partnerships with plants and other insects.

LEAF-CUTTING ANTS get their name from their habit of cutting and carrying off slices of leaves to their underground nests, where these are pressed into a heap that becomes a fungus garden. The ants then dine on the fungus that grows in this mass of dead vegetation. Nests are usually found in the forest, and the ants regularly climb trees there to harvest leaves. The various castes of leaf-cutting ants range in size from very tiny to an inch (2 to 20 mm). The "media" workers, which transport the leaves, are the most visible members of this species—less than half an inch (10 mm) in length. Leaf-cutting ants are found in Central and South America. A few species are even found in the U.S. Southwest and Northeast.

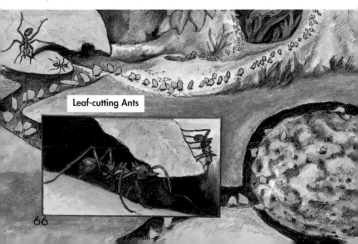

Leaf-cutting Ants

AZTECA ANTS, also called Cecropia Ants, include a handful of tiny (less than a quarter of an inch), brownish Central American rainforest species that form a mutually beneficial, or symbiotic, relationship with some Cecropia trees. These trees grow in the dense vegetation of light gaps and along the forest edges, where there is an intense struggle among the seedlings for sunlight and space. *Cecropia* saplings that are colonized by Azteca queens are more likely to survive. Ant colonies grow inside the young tree's hollow stem or trunk, and the ants dine on tiny droplets of sweetish fluids secreted by special glands in the leaves. In exchange for this service, the ants use their powerful jaws to prune or clip away any vines trying to wind their way up the tree trunk. The colony usually remains with the tree as it matures.

Azteca Ants

GIANT TROPICAL ANTS are the largest of the "ponerine" ants, with workers growing to nearly an inch in length. Ponerine ants are large, chiefly carnivorous South and Central American insects with fierce stings. Many nest in rotting logs or large decaying plant debris inside tree holes or on branches. One species nests in the roots of Gavilan Trees and attacks leaf-cutting ants on the trunks of the trees at night. A few types of ponerine ants, such as *Odontomachus*, have long, sickle-like jaws that snap open and shut. Pitch black in color, Giant Tropical Ants often attack and kill other rainforest insects and carry them back to their nests at the base of trees for food. They also collect plant nectar.

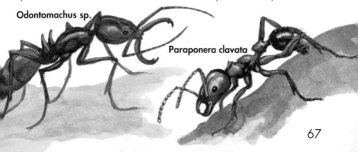

Odontomachus sp.

Paraponera clavata

67

Army ants

Pheidole ants

ARMY ANTS of over 150 different species are found from the southern United States to northern Argentina. Colonies of army ants can number over 1 million. The largest caste, the soldier ants, are about half an inch in length and have large mandibles. Army ants feed on other insects, including other ant species. Prey can include paper wasp brood, obtained by raids on nests in trees and buildings. All army ants are nomadic. Large troops in search of food move in columns, which is how they get their name. Some species lack eyes and rely instead on smell.

PHEIDOLE ANTS are the most common carnivorous insects found both in the leaf litter on the ground and the canopy overhead. There may be almost 600 species. These tiny ants (less than an eighth of an inch long) feed on arthropods such as orbatid mites and springtails, tiny creatures that decompose dead or dying plants in tropical rainforests.

Acacia ants

ACACIA ANTS are reddish brown and grow to roughly a quarter of an inch long. The female lays her eggs in a hollowed-out thorn of an acacia tree. The resulting colony remains in the tree, with the females leaving to start new colonies, sometimes searching for up to a month for a nesting place. Colonies can survive for more than 20 years. A single colony, occupying a single tree, may contain 70,000 individual ants. Acacia ants also obtain nourishment from their host trees, which form small fruiting bodies on the leaves. In exchange, the ants attack and kill other insects and sting livestock attempting to feed on the tree's foliage. Familiar ant-occupied acacias include the swollen thorns of Central American dry forests.

68

Bees and Wasps

Rainforests worldwide are home to thousands of bee and wasp species. Bees and wasps are closely related to ants. There are many different kinds of bees and wasps, most of which are active during daylight hours. In Central America, for example, some bees are active at night.

Powerfully built with strong wing muscles, bees carry pollen long distances and pollinate plants of the same species far from the original site. Because bees rear their own broods, they hunt not only to feed themselves but to provide food for their young in carefully crafted nests.

ORCHID BEES are best known for pollinating orchids, although they collect pollen and nectar from a wide variety of flowers. In some species both the male and female are large and black, with circles of pale yellow and red around their abdomens, but most species are metallic green, blue, or bronze. Their bodies are sometimes furry, and their wings are dark near the base and lighter at the tips. Orchid bees are found from tropical South America to southern Mexico. The females build nests in dead trees or in the ground, using mud to make small compartments. They usually collect this mud while the males, trying to attract the females, buzz around them in characteristic pattern, giving off a scent made from the fragrant chemicals in orchids.

Orchid bees

TRIGONA BEES, also often called Stingless Bees, form large colonies in Central America, southern Mexico, and northern South America. Black with orange abdomens and about a quarter-inch in length, they lack a sting as a defense mechanism and must protect themselves using their mandibles. Trigona Bees are active in daytime, collecting nesting materials as well as pollen and nectar from flowers. Though they typically swarm out of the nest by the thousands at dawn, they are usually observed working alone.

Trigona Bees

Carpenter Bees

CARPENTER BEES sculpt their nests out of wood, most often from dead branches or tree trunks. Tropical species are found throughout Mexico, Central America, and South America and resemble bumblebees. Females and males are roughly the same size (ranging from 1 to $1\frac{1}{4}$ inches), but the males have a tan, furry appearance while the females are shiny and black. Carpenter Bees tend to work and nest alone rather than in colonies, and only the females seem to collect nectar and pollen from flowers. Still, these strong-flying bees play an important role in transporting pollen from one tree to another of the same species.

PAPER WASPS are highly social insects identified by the structures of their nests, which are honeycomb compartments (cells) built of chewed wood "paper." Some species, such as those of the genus *Polistes*, build simple, uncovered nests with a single layer of cells. Others, such as those of the genus *Polybia*, build cylinder- or cone-shaped covered nests with several layers of cells. Paper wasps can be found throughout Mexico and Central and South America. Most *Polistes* are about an inch long, have elongated transparent or translucent wings, and have either dark brown, black, or colorfully striped bodies. *Polybia* wasps are less than half an inch long. Two of the three species are black with yellow markings; the third is entirely black. All paper wasps feed on caterpillars, termites, and other arthropods, which they catch, sting, and carry back to their nests to feed to their young.

Paper Wasps

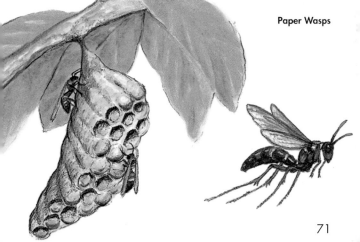

71

Other Insects

CARTON NEST TERMITES are a primitive group of insects that live in Central and South America. Their large, round nests, constructed in trees, are made from chewed wood cemented together, using the feces of the workers. About $\frac{1}{4}$ inch long, carton nest termites feed on decaying plant material and dead wood.

Giant Damselfly

Carton Nest Termites

GIANT DAMSELFLIES all have long, narrow bodies; slender, clear wings with deep blue stripes; and 7-inch wingspans. Because each of their four separate wings can move at different tempos, these insects are sometimes referred to as helicopter damselflies. Their bodies are quite thin and about 4 inches in length. Although they are too large to fly at high speeds, they are nimble enough to avoid capture. For this reason, they are usually observed from a distance. Giant Damselflies are found in Mexico, Central America, and northern South America. They feed mostly on spiders, which they capture in the spiders' webs. Giant damselflies often breed in water-filled tank bromeliads and tree holes above the forest floor.

Other Arthropods

GOLD ORB WEAVER SPIDERS create circular yellow webs up to 20 inches across, either within small clearings or along paths where there is enough sunlight to attract flying insects. Each web contains one female and several males, although webs may be joined together to form a colony. Females are about 1 inch long, much larger than males, and kill their trapped prey with a bite. Giant Damselflies will often pluck the carcasses of insects from the spiderwebs and feed on them.

Gold orb weaver spider

Large Forest-Floor Millipedes

LARGE FOREST-FLOOR MILLIPEDES are about 4 inches long and ½ inch wide, with brown striped bodies that are divided into 20 ivory-colored sections. Usually found in mating pairs, nests are built in the ground, and the young molt several times before reaching adulthood. Large Forest-floor Millipedes scavenge in the forest leaf litter, eating mostly rotting plant debris and decaying wood and expelling nutrients that act as a natural, nourishing fertilizer for the soil. Their main form of defense is a liquid they spray at foes; a frightened, curled-up millipede can squirt this toxic chemical up to a foot away.

73

REPTILES AND AMPHIBIANS

REPTILES ARE COLD-BLOODED, a classification that has less to do with actual body temperature than with the method these animals use to regulate body heat. Unlike birds and mammals, both of which are descended from reptilian ancestors, reptiles are unable to control body heat through internal processes and instead rely on absorbing external sources, such as sunlight or residual heat from the ground. This restricts most reptiles to regions with relatively warm climates, though if outside temperatures get too high, many reptiles will enter a state of half-sleep known as torpor. Familiar types of reptiles include turtles, snakes, lizards, chameleons, alligators, and crocodiles. The most notable physical feature of reptiles is their skin, which is covered with scales and often greenish in color.

Tropical rainforests have an especially rich assortment of reptiles, from spectacular species of snakes such as the

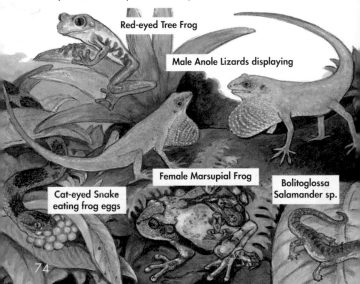

Red-eyed Tree Frog

Male Anole Lizards displaying

Female Marsupial Frog

Bolitoglossa Salamander sp.

Cat-eyed Snake eating frog eggs

Rainbow and Emerald Tree Boas to Komodo Dragons, Caiman Crocodiles, and Green Water Dragons. Some species of rainforest reptiles, such as the Flying Lizard, have even taken to the air, though their "flight" is more of a graceful glide from tree limb to tree limb than the true flight of birds.

Closely related to reptiles are the amphibians, from which the reptiles descended. Amphibians include frogs, toads, salamanders, and newts. Because amphibians must lay their eggs in a moist environment, most species must remain in warm, wet climates of the sort provided by the rainforests. Amphibians feed on insects and other arthropods.

One spectacular group of rainforest amphibians are the tree frogs. Although tree frogs are also found in various climates, they are extremely diversified in tropical rainforests. Several related species, for example, may exhibit unusual mating or breeding habits. During the night the calls of some rainforest tree frogs fill the air with a loud musical chorus of song.

Panther Chameleon

Flying Gecko

Tomato Frog

Green Mamba

Turtles

Turtles are reptiles with wide, flat bodies and patterned shells that are actually part of their skeleton. The top shell, called the carapace, covers the turtle's back. The shell beneath the body is called the plastron. Most turtles can withdraw their head, limbs, and tail entirely into their shell. Tropical rainforests support many species of land-dwelling turtles, which eat mostly insects. There are also some freshwater and tropical marine species that breed on beaches bordering rainforests.

GREEN TURTLES, found in warm ocean waters worldwide, come ashore mostly to breed. At night females crawl onto the beaches to lay their eggs in the sand. Hawks or other large birds may prey on the young turtles as they head to sea right after hatching. Green Turtles eat crustaceans, sponges, jellyfish, and submerged vegetation. Their shells measure up to 5 feet in length, and they have large, flipperlike legs that propel them rapidly through the water. The carapace is usually dark brown or green.

Green Turtle

MALAYAN SNAIL-EATING TURTLES
take their name from their diet,
which consists mostly of mollusks.
The carapace is dark brown and
grows up to 14 inches in length.
There is a distinctive yellow stripe
on the Malayan's face and neck.
This turtle is found in Southeast
Asia.

Malayan Snail Eating Turtle

MATAMATA TURTLES are strange-
looking, 2-foot-long South American
turtles, with flat heads atop thick
necks and tiny eyes surrounding a
thin, pointed snout. Leaflike flaps of
skin sit next to the turtle's head, and
the orangish top shell is sharply
ridged. Matamatas live in muddy
lakes, marshes, and slow-moving
backwater streams and eat fish and
aquatic invertebrates. They like to
ambush prey, striking out suddenly.

Matamata Turtle

Snakes

Snakes are rather odd reptiles. They lack any appendages on their outer bodies, though some primitive species have the vestigial remains of legs from earlier in their evolution. All snakes eat other animals, from ants and termites to storks, deer, and crocodiles. Most snakes have sharp teeth, to catch and swallow prey. In some species fangs are used to inject venom from special glands into small reptiles, birds, and mammals. The venom can paralyze or even kill prey, often quite swiftly. Other snakes kill by suffocating their prey.

BOA CONSTRICTORS attack their victims not by using poison but by winding their bodies in tight coils around unsuspecting prey, including lizards, birds, and some mammals, such as rodents. The average Boa Constrictor is less than 10 feet long, although some are longer and a few may reach 15 feet. Boa Constrictors are found from Mexico to tropical South America and from Paraguay to Argentina. They have one of the widest distributions of any snake.

Boa
Constrictor

EMERALD TREE BOAS are related to Boa Constrictors. They live primarily in the trees of the rainforest, where they either hang from the branches or flatten out against them. Slow-moving, these snakes dine mostly on rodents and grow to approximately 4 feet long. They are found from Guyana south to Brazil and Bolivia.

Brown Vine Snake

Emerald Tree Boa

VINE SNAKES are long, thin, green or brown snakes that blend neatly into the vines entangling the tree limbs where they spend most of their time. Their diet consists mainly of small lizards, but they will sometimes eat small birds and mammals. Vine snakes have a thin head and mild but nevertheless poisonous venom. If the snake feels threatened, the front part of its body puffs up in a formidable display. Vine snakes may grow to more than 6 feet long and are found in the United States, Mexico, and Central and South Americas.

79

FER-DE-LANCES are renowned for the extreme potency of their venom. Found from northern Mexico to Argentina, they live in both rainforests and open country. The distinctive crosshatched pattern on the snake's body is dark gray and tan. Fer-de-Lances belong to the Pit Viper family and have the characteristic triangular heads. They eat frogs, lizards, and small to medium-sized rodents. Lengths of 8 feet or more have been reported for these snakes.

South American Rattlesnake

Fer-de-Lance

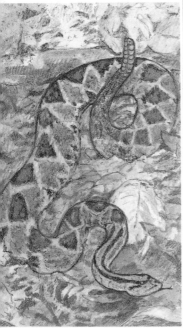

SOUTH AMERICAN RATTLESNAKES are the most widely distributed species of rattlesnake, occurring in Mexico, Central America, and all of South America except Ecuador and Chile. However, they live primarily in semiarid regions and are rarely found in rainforests. Probably the most dangerous of all rattlesnakes, they emit or eject a deadly venom that can cause quick paralysis and even death. Rodents are their primary prey. About 1½ feet long, these rattlesnakes have small heads and yellow or pale olive skin with brown patterns on it.

EYELASH VIPERS, which are relatives of Fer-de-lances, also belong to the pit viper family and are found from Mexico south to Colombia, Venezuela, and Ecuador. Close to 2 feet in length, they come in several color patterns, including olive green with black and reddish spots and yellowish green with brown spots. One variety is almost completely black, with the tip of the tail red. Mostly nocturnal, Eyelash Vipers spend much of their time hanging from tree limbs by their tails. These snakes were named for the flaplike scales that extend out above their eyes and resemble eyelashes.

Eyelash Viper

Gaboon Viper

GABOON VIPERS grow to more than 5 feet long. Found in West and South Africa, south of the Sahara Desert, the Gaboon Viper has a slender neck, a wide head, very long fangs, and a thin tail. Gaboon Vipers eat a wide variety of vertebrates, including frogs, lizards, large rodents, and birds. Their venom can cause paralysis and death. They breed every two to three years, producing up to 60 young per litter.

BUSHMASTERS are the largest of the Pit Vipers. There is only one species of this snake. Shy during the day, it hides inside hollow trees and small caves until nightfall, at which time it comes out to feed, primarily on rodents. Although its venom is less poisonous than some, it produces prodigious quantities of it, making it one of the deadliest snakes on Earth. Found in southern Central America and the Amazonian Basin of South America, Bushmasters can grow to be more than 11 feet long.

Coral Snake

Bushmaster

CORAL SNAKES are generally small but strikingly colored snakes, with bright red, yellow, and black bands. Along with large cobras and death adders, they belong to the group called elapid snakes. Corals are often found prowling around the outsides of buildings. Because these snakes are very poisonous, their bold color patterns are mimicked by some other, nonpoisonous species as a means of protection from snake enemies such as hawks. Common in Central American rainforests, Coral Snakes eat other snakes and other small reptiles such as Anole Lizards.

Crocodilians

The crocodilians, which include the crocodiles, alligators, and caimans, are living fossils. They are the only surviving members—except perhaps birds—of a class of reptiles known as the archosaurs, the dominant land animals of the Mesozoic era of more than 60 million years ago. This class also included among its ranks the now-extinct dinosaurs and flying reptiles. Crocodilians are found in the tropics and subtropics and are among the largest of living reptiles.

SPECTACLED CAIMANS occur from Venezuela to the Amazon Basin. They take their name from the ridge that runs between their eyes, giving these reptiles the appearance of wearing glasses. Reaching lengths of 6 or 7 feet, they eat invertebrates, other reptiles, small mammals, and birds. Because of overhunting for their valuable skins, their numbers have declined in recent years.

Spectacled Caiman

Estuarine Crocodile

ESTUARINE CROCODILES are among the largest (up to 20 feet long) and most dangerous crocodiles. Also called Saltwater Crocodiles, they spend most of their time in water, in Indonesia and Australia, looking for fish, reptile, and bird prey. Their hides are used to make leather; thus the species is rapidly being exterminated by hunters.

Other Reptiles

COMMON IGUANAS are found from Mexico to Central and South America. They live mostly in trees, where they eat plants. Identified by the spines running from neck to tail, they also have across their back colored bands that darken with age. Iguanas can grow to over 6 feet long, including the tail. Also called Green Iguanas, these reptiles are hunted by humans for their flesh and eggs and are also popular today as pets.

Common Iguana

Flying Dragon

FLYING DRAGONS live in the trees of Indonesian rainforests, gliding from branch to branch with the help of skin flaps connected to their limbs. Reaching lengths of about 8 inches, the Flying Dragon is carnivorous and feeds mostly on insects.

GREEN WATER DRAGONS, also known as Thai Water Dragons, have a saillike crest on their heads. Although they live in trees, Green Water Dragons are capable of running on top of the water with the aid of fringes on their hind feet. Reaching lengths of more than 3 feet, they are found in New Guinea and the surrounding areas and eat chiefly insects and frogs.

Green Water Dragon

Madagascaar Leaf-tailed Gecko

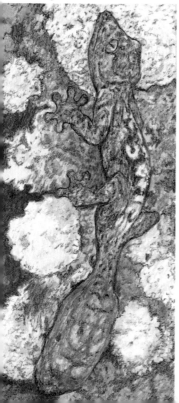

MADAGASCAR LEAF-TAILED GECKOS can change color to blend into tree bark. (All geckos can darken or lighten their skin to fit into their surroundings.) Found only on the island of Madagascar, these geckos have flat bodies and grow to about 8 inches in length. They probably eat a variety of invertebrates and small vertebrates.

85

WHITE-BELLIED WORM LIZARDS are not lizards but are in the same order. With their cylindrical bodies and blunt tails and heads, they are sometimes mistaken for snakes. They live in underground burrows, though they will sometimes emerge during rainstorms. More than an inch in diameter and roughly 2 feet in length, they are found in South America and Trinidad.

White-bellied Worm Lizard

COMMON TEGUS are large South American lizards with strong legs and long tails. They live in open areas and at the forest edge. Their diet includes invertebrates, small vertebrates, and birds' eggs. They grow to lengths of 3 to 5 feet, including the tail, and their skin is dark brown or black in color.

Common Tegus

KOMODO DRAGONS can grow to lengths of over 10 feet and can weigh over 200 pounds. They are the largest of the modern lizards. Carnivores, they prey on large animals such as deer and pigs and occasionally attack people. Found in Indonesia, the Komodo Dragon has jagged teeth and a forked tongue. It can climb trees and swim.

Komodo Dragon

Double-crested Basilisk

DOUBLE-CRESTED BASILISKS are found in Central America. Their skin is green with yellow or blue spots. The males are identified by their large crests. Growing to lengths of more than 2 feet, Double-crested Basilisks can run very fast—across both ground and water—when fleeing from a predator or chasing prey. Because they can walk on water, they have become popularly known as "Jesus Christ" Lizards.

87

Frogs and Toads

Frogs have the widest geographical distribution of all amphibians. Best known for the jumping power of their long hind legs, adult frogs have no tails, and their tongues, attached at the front rather than the back of their mouths, can be flicked outward to catch prey. Although tadpoles eat mostly plants and insects, large adult frogs dine on a variety of animals, including mice, birds, and fish.

Toads are actually a type of frog that is more resistant to water loss than other frogs. The name "toad" really refers to frogs of the family Bufonidae but is often applied to any frog that has shortish legs and a squat, warty appearance. True toads prefer a drier environment than most other amphibians. A few species live their entire lives out of the water and incubate their eggs on their backs.

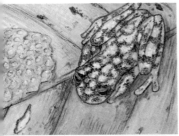

GLASS FROGS have green-tinted, nearly transparent skin that their organs almost show through. Quite small, these species of frog reach only about an inch in length and are found in Central and South America.

ORNATE HORNED FROGS have bright green skin that is covered with brown and black spots. Their plump, roundish bodies grow to a length of about 5 inches. Found in South America, mostly in Argentina and Brazil, these frogs have strong jaws and are vicious predators. They feed on other amphibians, small mammals, and invertebrates.

STRAWBERRY POISON-DART FROGS are members of a large group of frog species that all secrete poison from skin glands. Some Indian tribes in the Americas use this poison on their arrowheads. Many poison-dart frogs breed in rainwater-filled tank bromeliads, where their tadpoles eat small aquatic insects. Parent frogs carry tadpoles from one bromeliad to another for fresh water and food. The name "strawberry" comes from the frog's speckled reddish orange warning coloration. At lengths of up to 1 inch, the frogs cling to leaves and trees, using tiny adhesive disks on their toes. Poison-dart frogs are found in Central America. Another striking poison-dart frog is the black-and-green *Dendrobates auratus*.

Strawberry Poison-Dart Frog

Dendrobates auratus

WALLACE'S FLYING FROGS, in spite of their name, are not capable of true flight. Like other gliding animals, these frogs have flaps of skin attached to their limbs that allow them to glide from tree to tree. Identified by their long legs and the extensive webbing between their toes and fingers, they grow to lengths of roughly 4 inches and are found in Southeast Asia.

Wallace's Flying Frog

MARINE TOADS are natives of southern Texas and northern South America. They are also known as Giant Toads and Mexican Toads and can grow to lengths of 9 inches. In the 1920s they were introduced into Puerto Rico, where they became known as Cane Toads. The female Marine Toad can lay as many as 35,000 eggs in a single year.

Marine Toad

GOLDEN TOADS are found only in the Costa Rican Monteverde Cloud Forest Reserve. About 2 inches in length, they live underground or in the aboveground roots of large trees, coming out only once a year to mate. Since 1989 no members of the species have been observed, and some experts believe they may now be extinct.

Golden Toads

SURINAM TOADS are not true toads but have their characteristic squat appearance. Typical members of the primitive *Pipa* genus, these toads rarely leave the water. Their hind legs splay out to both sides of their body, ending in broadly webbed feet that give these toads a strong swimming stroke. Their fingertips are equipped with tiny filaments that can be used to probe in the mud for food. About 6 to 8 inches long, their bodies are flat, and their beige or brown color helps camouflage them while in the mud. The triangular head narrows to a point at the nose. The eggs that are released by the female during mating are fertilized by the male, who attaches them to the female's back. The female's skin then thickens over the eggs to enclose them almost completely until they hatch a few months later.

Surinam Toad

MEXICAN BURROWING TOADS are the only known surviving members of the ancient Rhinophrynidae family of frogs. Also called Cone-nosed Toads, because of their small, pointy heads and egg-shaped bodies, they are about $3\frac{1}{2}$ inches long. Spadelike appendages extend from their hind feet and are used for digging out burrows. These toads live in holes in the ground, emerging to mate in rainwater ponds. Unusual for frogs, their tongues are slowly extended out of the mouth, rather than flicked at prey.

Mexican Burrowing Toad

BIRDS

ACCORDING TO ONE POPULAR THEORY, birds are the direct descendants of dinosaurs. Unquestionably, they are the descendants of some type of reptile that lived about 200 million years ago in the early Mesozoic era.

Birds are the only feathered animals. Although they are not the only animals that can fly, all living species of birds either can fly now or are descended from earlier species that could. Birds lay hard-shelled eggs in which the embryos of their young can develop outside the mother's body.

There are 27 different orders of birds. Nearly two-thirds of these fall into a single order, the Passeriformes, and are known as passerines or perching birds.

Although birds are found in every kind of environment, including the frigid Antarctic, the rainforest has a very diverse collection of species. Several closely related rainforest species might inhabit a common area but differ greatly in appearance and behavior and even have different songs.

Many tropical male birds have bright plumages that may help them locate mates in the shadows and dark color tones of the rainforest. Also, the beaks and bills of many tropical birds reflect that particular bird's specialized feeding habits.

Archaeopteryx,
the first bird, known only
from fossil remains.

Cassowaries

Cassowaries, now threatened, are large, powerful, flight-less birds with small wings, found in the wild only in Australia and Asia. They can run very fast and eat mostly fallen fruits from various rainforest vines and trees, as well as the occasional dead bird and mammal. Cassowaries need large tracts of rainforest habitat to forage for food.

DOUBLE-WATTLED CASSOWARIES, also called Southern Cassowaries, are 3 to 4 feet tall and are found in northern Australia, New Guinea, and eastern Indonesia. They are identified by the two bright red wattles that hang below their necks and the hard, curved "casques" mounted atop their heads like the crests on helmets. These structures may be used for clearing paths through dense forest brush as the birds search for the vegetation they like to eat. The nearly bald heads of these cassowaries are a bluish tone, and their body plumage is black. Their feet have sharp toes that can serve as weapons to protect the birds against enemies.

Double-wattled Cassowary

Herons

Herons (including bitterns and egrets) have long necks and wings. In the tropics they are seen mostly along streams, rivers, and open waterways, wading in or perching at the water's edge to nab fish or snakes with their sharp beaks. Some feed by day, others at night or dawn or dusk.

Rufescent Tiger-Heron

White-crested Bittern

RUFESCENT TIGER-HERONS, at about 2 feet tall, are named for the orange-and-black striped patterns on their plumage, which is reminiscent of the pelt of a tiger. They have loud, booming calls and live in swampy areas or streams inside Central and South American rainforests, from Honduras to northern Argentina. Rarely seen in the open during the day, they can stand motionless at the water's edge for very long periods, awaiting prey.

WHITE-CRESTED BITTERNS are 2-foot-tall herons found in tropical west Africa. They live largely solitary lives deep inside tropical forests, coming out mostly at night to feed.

CATTLE EGRETS are small herons with mostly white feathers, yellow bills, and a squatter, shorter neck than is typical for egrets. These birds, which are originally from Africa, like to roost in trees overhanging water and are found all over today, including Central and South America. The Cattle Egret feeds on insects that have often been stirred up by grazing cattle—hence, their name.

Cattle Egret

94

Birds of Prey

Birds of prey are found all over and include falcons, eagles, hawks, and vultures. Daytime hunters, these birds have powerful hooked beaks and sharp, curved claws and feed on snakes, rodents, bats, and other vertebrates. (See also p. 108 for nocturnally active birds of prey.) They perch in the forest canopy along breaks created by streams and light gaps, looking for prey below. All have keen eyesight. Most birds of prey nest in trees or on high cliffs. American rainforest vultures are distant cousins to the vultures of Africa. All are carrion feeders with a highly developed sense of smell, feet adapted for perching, and bald heads.

BARRED FOREST FALCONS are noted for their long legs and tails and short wings rounded at the tip. The colors and patterns of their plumage vary widely from place to place, with the range of the birds extending from Central to South America. A typical Barred Forest Falcon can be 13 to 15 inches long. Its short wings allow it to fly easily through the trees of the rainforest, where it can hide under cover to wait for its prey, usually other birds or small mammals.

Barred Forest
Falcon

95

CRESTED CARACARAS are fairly large birds closely related to falcons. The head of the Crested Caracara is white with a black crest. The neck is long. The body, which grows to about 2 feet in length and weighs about 20 pounds, is mostly black, with a white tail and yellow legs. Crested Caracaras feed on small animals, sometimes going after live frogs, snakes, rodents, and young birds. Their nests can often be found near the tops of palm trees.

Crested Caracara

Harpy Eagle

HARPY EAGLES can be found from southern Mexico to northern Argentina. These endangered birds are the largest eagles and very strong. About 3 feet tall with black-and-white plumage, they seem rather owllike in appearance. Their short wings are ideal for flying swiftly among branches in the forest in search of tree-dwelling prey such as large birds, sloths, coatis, porcupines, or monkeys. Their nests are platforms of sticks lined with leafy twigs and built in the forks of giant emergent trees such as kapoks.

KING VULTURES are found from Mexico to northern Argentina. These striking birds, nearly 3 feet tall, are easily identified by the mottled pattern of colors on their heads and beaks and their white-and-black plumage. Although common, King Vultures usually fly far above the treetops, making them hard to spot. They feed on both carrion and live prey and nest in low, hollow tree stumps or depressions in the forest floor.

King Vultures

BLACK VULTURES occur from the eastern United States to northern Chile and Argentina. They eat mostly carrion but will also eat rotten fruits and vegetables and kill and eat ducks, turtles, and small mammals. About 2 feet tall with all-black plumage and more gregarious than other vultures, they are often found near towns and cities. Vultures are the most conspicuous scavengers of the New World tropics. Because of them, carcasses and other carrion quickly disappear.

Black Vultures

Game Birds

Most game birds live on the ground, though a few live in trees. They tend to be plump and round, and many cannot fly. Pheasants, including turkeys and quails, are probably the most familiar game birds. They eat mostly seeds but also insects and berries. Many tropical game birds have very elaborate courtship displays, with certain sounds and postures they use to attract mates. But because they are easy prey and hunted for food and sport, game-bird populations in the tropics have dwindled dramatically in recent years.

GREAT CURRASOWS live both in the trees and on the ground, feeding on the fruit and berries they find there. They have very loud, booming calls and are believed by some to use ventriloquism, because it is difficult to tell which direction their calls are coming from. Found in tropical rainforests from Mexico to Ecuador, they grow to lengths of more than 3 feet. But these birds are rapidly disappearing from the rainforests with the encroachment of civilization.

Great Currassows

MALAY GREAT ARGUS PHEASANTS are shy, long-lived birds (typically 30 years) that are difficult to spot. They are found in Indonesia, from the Malay Peninsula to Sumatra. Although they have been seen in the rainforest, they usually prefer drier regions. The males are large, with a body length of up to 3 feet and a wingspan of about 6 feet. The females are smaller, about 2 feet in length with a wingspan of about 1½ feet. The heads of these birds are blue, with a crown of black feathers and a thin mane of feathers on the neck. The back feathers are yellow with black spots. During the mating season the males dance and display their feathers, like peacocks.

Malay Great Argus Pheasant

Congo Peacock

CONGO PEACOCKS, at about 40 inches long including the tail, are the largest African game birds. Very secretive, these pheasants are found mostly in central Africa, where they hide in the trees. The males have dark plumages and a dark feathered head crest; the females have bright green feathers on their backs.

99

Rails and Sunbitterns

BLACK RAILS are among a number of Central and South American rainforest rail species. Related to cranes, coots, and gallinules, all rails are adapted for life in thick vegetation. Their thin bodies allow them to squeeze easily through tangled undergrowth to avoid predators. Rails are very secretive, hiding out in flooded pastures or grassy marshes and scurrying under vegetation when disturbed. Most species have brown, gray, or black plumage with spots or streaks; the sexes look alike. Small invertebrates, berries, and seeds are dug up in the soft mud or leaf litter and eaten. Some species are active on moonlit nights, though they are day-flying birds. Perhaps because they hide so well, these birds have become rather solitary; a few species are now even flightless.

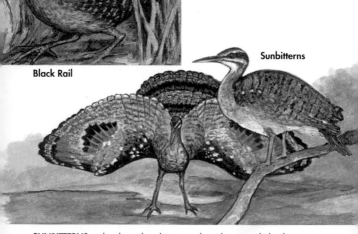

Black Rail

Sunbitterns

SUNBITTERNS, closely related to rails, live along stream banks on the edges of Central and South American rainforests, where the variegated patterns of their plumages make them difficult to see. Only when threatened do they open up their wings fully, revealing striking coloration. Sunbitterns eat fish and insects, often wading into the water to catch prey.

Pigeons

Familiar to most city dwellers because some species like living close to humans, pigeons nonetheless occur widely around the world. A few species are found in rainforests.

NICOBAR PIGEONS, at about 15 inches long, have heavy bills and a vulturelike posture. Unlike more familiar pigeon species, Nicobars are long-legged and have short green plumage. Found in New Guinea, the Philippines, and the Solomon Islands area, these ground dwellers usually nest on smaller islands but travel in flocks to larger islands and coastal mainland rainforests to feed.

Nicobar Pigeon

Victoria Crowned Pigeon

VICTORIA CROWNED PIGEONS can reach lengths of about 2 feet. Found in and near Indonesia and northern New Guinea, they get their name from the fan-shaped feather crowns on their heads, which forms a lace-like latticework in both males and females. These pigeons spend a lot of time on the ground gathering berries and fruits or hiding in trees.

Parrots

For many people, parrots are the quintessential rainforest birds. And, indeed, there is a great variety of tropical and subtropical species. Because of their large size and tendency to travel in flocks, parrots can disperse large numbers of seeds, thus helping to shape the tropical landscape.

The parrot's feathers are usually brightly colored, and its versatile bill can be used for lifting, climbing, and feeding. The loud squawking of parrots is one of the noisiest sounds in the rainforest. Oddly, the ability of some parrots to mimic sounds is seen only in captivity.

Scarlet Macaw

SCARLET MACAWS are strikingly colored parrots. They are also long-lived birds, many reaching 90 years of age. Their plumages, mainly a vivid red, are accented by yellows, greens, blues, and other shades. Alas, the loss of the Scarlet Macaw's habitat and capture of young birds for sale to collectors has greatly reduced its numbers in the wild. Found both in rainforests and open savannas from Mexico to Brazil, this bird eats a variety of fruits and seeds and grows to nearly 3 feet in length.

RAINBOW LORIKEETS (LORIES) are found in rainforests and open parklands in New Guinea, Australia, and Indonesia. About 11 inches in length, they have beautiful multicolored plumages that give the bird its name. Unlike most other rainforest species, Rainbow Lories like to live near human beings and are often seen in flocks of 100 or more. They have a varied diet of flowers, leaves, berries, seeds, and grain crops, which causes them to be thought of as pests in farming regions.

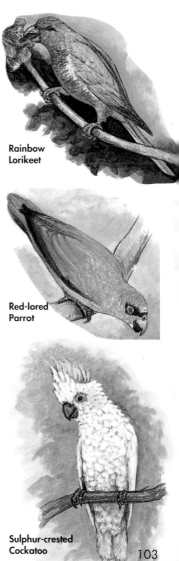

Rainbow Lorikeet

RED-LORED PARROTS occur from eastern Mexico to western Ecuador and central Brazil. About 1 foot long and weighing only about 1 pound, their bodies are mostly green, with bluish crowns and patches of yellow on the neck. Patches of blue and red are also visible, along with yellow stripes on their tails. Unusual for parrots, these birds prefer to stay within a small area of the rainforest and nest in the holes of tall, dead trees, feeding on palm and other seeds and fruits such as figs in the upper branches of rainforest trees.

Red-lored Parrot

SULPHUR-CRESTED COCKATOOS, like all cockatoos, have rather large, upward-pointing crests of feathers on their heads. The Sulphur's crest is mostly white fringed with yellow. The males are more brightly colored than the females. These parrots, which perch on dead, emergent trees in noisy flocks at dawn and dusk, feed on grass seed or berries. Also found in swamps, mangroves, and palm and eucalyptus forests, they are hunted as pests by Australian farmers.

Sulphur-crested Cockatoo

103

Toucans and Woodpeckers

Toucans and woodpeckers both belong to the Piciformes order of birds. Toucans are native to Central and South America. They are large, brightly colored birds with unusually large beaks—in some cases longer than the rest of their bodies. Woodpeckers are noted for their sharp, pointed bills, which they use to find and nab insect prey in bark, and their ability to cling to the sides of trees. They are found in many environments and on all continents except Australia.

KEEL-BILLED TOUCANS are among the largest and most colorful of the toucans, growing to nearly 2 feet in length. Found from Mexico to Venezuela, members of this species travel in small flocks and eat fruits, insects, and some small animals. In Central America they dine on the long, dangling fruits of Cecropia trees located along rainforest edges. Near sunset, small groups of these stunning birds often can be seen perched on these trees, emitting their characteristic "creaky-gate" calls.

Keel-billed Toucan

Fiery-billed Aracari

FIERY-BILLED ARACARIS live in the canopy levels of Costa Rican and Panamanian rainforests. They have green bodies about $1\frac{1}{2}$ feet long and black heads and chests. Their rumps and tails are red. Their bills are orange or vermilion on the upper mandible and black on the lower mandible, and the base is outlined in white.

ACORN WOODPECKERS are found from the western United States to Colombia. They live in forests and clearings with scattered dead trees, in groups of three to six. Excavating hundreds of regularly spaced holes in wood or amid epiphytes in which they store acorns, these 8-inch-long birds are also expert fly catchers.

Pale-billed Woodpecker

Acorn Woodpecker

PALE-BILLED WOODPECKERS prefer to live in the middle to upper levels of the rainforest. They dig deeply into the bark of decaying trunks, eating mostly wood-boring beetles and their larvae (though they will also eat some fruit). This hastens the decay of these trees, especially in light gaps and other small clearings, and thus helps recycle the nutrients they contain. About 14 inches long, these birds are found from northern Mexico to western Panama.

105

Kingfishers and Hornbills

Kingfishers, which nest in ground holes, have large heads and short, stout bodies. Many species have sharp beaks used for spearing fish, though—despite their name—not all eat fish. Some have hooked beaks and eat insects. Hornbills are found exclusively in the Old World. Members of this family have large, strong, downward-curving bills with nearly hollow casques on top. They feed mainly on fruit and invertebrates. Although the two groups are not close relatives, hornbills do resemble toucans and have similar nesting habits.

Ringed Kingfisher

RINGED KINGFISHERS, at about 16 inches long, have bushy crests and long, stout bills. They prefer to stay near smooth-flowing, deep lowland streams and dive for fish from the overhanging branches. Found in southern Texas to Tierra del Fuego and the Lesser Antilles, they nest in burrows on the banks of the streams.

RHINOCEROS HORNBILLS, which are found in Indonesia, have black plumages with white bellies and white tails with black bands. The bills of these birds are large and yellow, with upturned casques on top. The male is 4 feet in length, the female 3 feet. Both sexes nest in hollow trees, but when the female nests, she seals herself into the hole, using her own droppings, and remains there until her young are born. She eats by sticking her bill through a small pecked-out hole and taking food the male brings her.

Rhinoceros Hornbill

Cuckoos

Cuckoos are found all over, in many different types of environments, and are named for the sound made by the European Cuckoo. Some species lay their eggs in nests of other birds, tossing out the hosts' eggs. The unaware foster parents raise the baby cuckoos instead of their own offspring.

SQUIRREL CUCKOOS, at about 18 inches long, usually nest in the forest canopy. Flying only short distances, these cuckoos stay mostly on the ground, hunting for food or leaping from tree to tree and running along the branches like squirrels. Found from Mexico to Argentina, they feed on insects, small lizards, and small mammals such as mice. They have chestnut-colored feathers on their heads and backs, black rumps, and grayish chests.

Squirrel Cuckoo

Rufous-vented Ground-cuckoo

RUFOUS-VENTED GROUND-CUCKOOS live on the damp forest floor singly, in pairs, or in small groups. They will often forage at army-ant raids. They also eat large insects, scorpions, centipedes, spiders, small frogs and lizards, and even fruit. Found from northeastern Nicaragua to eastern Peru, Bolivia, and central Brazil, they are about 19 inches long.

Owls

Owls are carnivorous, like other raptors. However, unlike hawks and falcons, they prefer to hunt at dusk or in the dark and have eyes that face forward rather than to the side. They feed on insects, mice, and even animals as large as rabbits and have small, strong beaks and sharp claws. Not surprisingly, both their night vision and hearing are highly developed, and they can swivel their heads nearly all the way around when searching for prey.

SPECTACLED OWLS, from southern Mexico to western Ecuador, Bolivia, and northern Argentina, reside in dense forest areas but hunt in clearings or along the edges of forests. They are about 19 inches long and spend most of their time in the trees just under the forest canopy, feeding on small mammals, lizards, birds, crabs, or even large insects. Spectacled Owls were named for the markings around their eyes, which make it appear as though they are wearing glasses.

Spectacled Owls

Passerines

Passerines make up the majority of birds on Earth. They are the "perching" birds, so called because their four-toed feet are adapted for holding onto branches. Most familiar bird species, such as wrens, crows, swallows, jays, sparrows, cardinals, bluebirds, and robins, are passerines. Ornithologists sometimes divide passerines into two groups: true passerines and other songbirds (including thrushes and larks).

Long-tailed Manakin

LONG-TAILED MANAKINS live on small berries plucked without the bird alighting. Between about 5 and 10 inches long and found mostly in western Central America from Mexico to Costa Rica, the birds live both in thickets and on tree branches. The striking male has a red crown, blue back, orange legs, and long tail feathers. Males gather in groups called leks and "sing" to attract females.

Three-wattled Bellbird

THREE-WATTLED BELLBIRDS are a Central American species with a call sometimes described as explosive because of its loudness. Males are about 1 foot long; females are a bit shorter. Living in the upper reaches of trees, Bellbirds are difficult to spot but easy to hear. Their bills are large enough to grab whole fruits, which is what they mostly feed on.

BARE-NECKED UMBRELLABIRDS are found in the understory and canopy levels of Costa Rican and Panamanian rainforests. Their large bills are black, and their heads have umbrella-like crests. The male, about 16 inches long, has a glossy blue-black coat and bare, bright orange throat skin. The smaller female is also black but less glossy. These birds eat palm fruits and other plants, large insects such as katydids, and small frogs or lizards. They may beat their prey against a branch before swallowing it. Displaying males emit a deep, booming sound using a neck sac that inflates, then deflates as the sound fades.

Bare-necked Umbrellabird

White-throated Magpie Jay

WHITE-THROATED MAGPIE JAYS are large blue-and-white jays with long tails and large crests of white to black feathers. Their bodies have mostly blue and black feathers. Found from Mexico to Costa Rica, they search for food, including fruits, insects, and small lizards, in thick foliage and can travel many miles in a day, visiting many fruiting trees.

TENNESSEE WARBLERS winter from Mexico to northern South America, when their plumages are olive green above and white below, with yellowish breasts and gray heads. Their sharp bills, which they use to eat mostly spiders, mistletoe and other berries, and flower nectar, can be over 4 inches long.

Tennessee Warbler

CANADA WARBLERS breed in North America but winter in both Central and South America, hovering in the air while plucking insects off leaves and twigs. Reaching lengths of about 5 inches, they have gray feathers on their backs with yellow underparts. One of about 110 species of warblers (nearly all North American), Canada Warblers and related species are not highly integrated into the rainforest ecosystem.

Canada Warbler

MONTEZUMA OROPENDOLAS are found from Mexico to Panama. They have black heads and chests, maroon bodies, and usually nest in very dense colonies in isolated trees or clearings but forage for seeds, fruits, insects, and small invertebrates in the canopy. At about 20 inches long, males are a bit larger than females. Cowbirds often lay their eggs in Oropendola nests; the baby cowbirds acquire a baby-sitter but help protect the Oropendola chicks by eating the larvae of life-threatening bot flies.

Montezuma Oropendolas

111

Trogons

Quetzals, found from Mexico to Nicaragua, are probably the best-known trogons in the rainforest. The national bird of Guatemala, their name comes from an Aztec word meaning "beautiful." Although small in size, most male quetzals have vivid red bellies; the rest of the body is green. The bright green feathers on the heads and necks of both males and females serve to camouflage the birds as they sit in the trees. Quetzals can remain motionless for a long time, especially if they sense intruders. They spend most of their lives in the rainforest canopy but make their nests lower down, in decaying tree stumps.

RESPLENDENT QUETZALS are about 14 inches in length and live in forest canopies from Mexico to Panama. The males have up to 2-foot-long streamers on their tails and helmet-like crests on their heads that extend forward to cover their bills. Their bodies are iridescent green, with maroon and crimson breasts and yellow bills. The females are less colorful. Resplendent Quetzals feed on fruits, insects, and small animals, including frogs and snails. They live in decaying trees and are currently endangered.

Resplendent
Quetzals

Hummingbirds

Found only in the New World, hummingbirds are small (2 to 8 inches in length), colorful, iridescent birds with long bills, rapid wing beats, and distinct flight patterns. Related to swifts and swallows, most of the 330 hummingbird species live in the tropics, where they sip nectar—usually from reddish or orange tubular flowers—while hovering in the air. They also pluck insects and spiders from foliage. Important rainforest pollinators, hummingbirds build tiny cups of soft fibers for nests and decorate them with mosses and lichens.

Long-tailed Hermit

Violet Sabrewings

White-crested Coquettes

LONG-TAILED HERMITS live in rainforest understories from Mexico to Brazil, where the 6-inch-long birds hide in the shadows—hence the name "hermit." Their long, curved bills are useful for sucking nectar from Heliconias and other rainforest flowers and nabbing insects.

VIOLET SABREWINGS prefer to live in the understory along streams and woods. One of their favorite foods is bananas. Up to ten males may form a lek, singing from tree saplings along the forest's edge. Found from southern Mexico to western Panama, these humming-birds are about 6 inches long.

WHITE-CRESTED COQUETTES are less than 3 inches long, and the male has an ornate crest and cheek tufts. These Central American birds live high up in the canopy. They appear only when the Inga and certain other rainforest flowers are in bloom. Then they disappear again.

MAMMALS

MAMMALS ARE WARM-BLOODED animals that produce milk to feed their young and have body hair. Of all animals, mammals are probably of the greatest interest to people—because people are mammals. Large mammals, such as gorillas, tigers, and pandas, are perennial favorites in public zoos. Because they require relatively substantial habitats to support their lifestyles, large mammals are relatively rare in rainforests compared to insects and plants. And many existing species are now in danger of extinction.

Mammals evolved from reptiles more than 200 million years ago, at the beginning of the Mesozoic era. But it was not until 65 million years ago that they came to dominate land environments, after the sudden extinction of most large Mesozoic dinosaurs.

Tree Pangolin (Africa)

Coati (Americas)

Mandrill (Africa)

Giant Otter (S. America)

Paca (Americas)

Marsupials

Marsupials, ranging from tiny shrewlike insectivores to large grass-eating kangaroos, are very primitive mammals, but they still thrive in South America (81 species), Australia (120 species), and New Guinea (53 species). Marsupials generally have a pouch, or marsupium. The babies, born early by "placental" mammal standards, crawl into this pouch, where they feed from a nipple and develop further. In a few New World species, the pouch has atrophied or vanished entirely.

SPOTTED CUSCUS, in spite of resembling monkeys, are really opossums. Found mostly in the mountainous areas of New Guinea, where they live in trees and eat fruits and insects, similar species of cuscus may inhabit non-overlapping ranges at different altitudes. Typical individuals are 1 to 2 feet long, with a prehensile tail often used as a third hand. Females have thick gray fur and a pouch; males are red with pale spots.

Spotted Cuscus

Virginia Opossum

VIRGINIA OPOSSUMS, though now widespread in the temperate areas of North America from which they derive their common name, evolved in the tropics and are still commonly found in the rainforests of Central America. Able to eat a wide variety of foods, they nest in tree hollows and can hang from branches by their tails. Typically about $1\frac{1}{2}$ feet in length, they have long muzzles and gray or brown fur.

TREE KANGAROOS are the only kangaroos found in rainforests. As their name implies, they dwell in the branches of trees. There are several species. Kangaroos are perhaps the best known of all marsupials. They eat leaves and fruits of various trees and shrubs and can be readily identified by their powerful limbs, stiff tails, and upright, leaping postures. Tree kangaroos tend to be smaller than most non-arboreal kangaroos, measuring only about 2 feet or so from head to toe, with equally long tails. Typically, the members of this genus feed at night and sleep on tree branches during the day. Like all other kangaroos, tree kangaroos are found only in Australia and New Guinea. Because their forelimbs are more highly developed than those of ground-dwelling kangaroos, tree kangaroos look somewhat apelike in appearance.

Tree Kangaroos

Insectivores and Tree Shrews

Insectivores are small, rather primitive nocturnal mammals that eat ants and other insects found in tree branches and on the ground. They are very active due to their small body size and high metabolic rate. Worldwide, their order includes hedgehogs, moles, and shrews. Tree shrews were once considered insectivores, but their bigger brains and larger eyes led scientists to create a separate family for them called Tupaiidae.

HISPANIOLA SOLENODONS are found on the island of Hispaniola in the West Indies. Before the Europeans came, solenodons were the dominant carnivores there and in Cuba, only occasionally falling prey to boas and birds of prey. Less than 2 feet long, Hispaniola Solenodons are nocturnal and have small brains and highly developed senses. They eat mainly invertebrates (insect larvae, earthworms, termites, beetles, crickets, and millipedes), all found in the soil and leaf litter.

TREE SHREWS look like squirrels, both in their bushy tails and the way they scurry up and down trees. But their pointed snouts are distinctly unsquirrel-like. Not related to true shrews, they are also not particularly suited to living in trees. Found in Indonesia and southern China, they are about 6 inches long, with equally long tails. Their fur is usually gray or brown with a whitish underside. Most species have large earflaps that enhance hearing. Though they nest in tree hollows, the shrews are usually on the ground looking for insects.

Hispaniola Solenodon

Tree Shrew

Colugos

The only members of the order Dermoptera are several species of flying lemurs called colugos. Flying lemurs are not related to the primates known as lemurs and are not capable of true flight. Probably more closely related to insectivores and some bats, flying lemurs are gliding mammals, moving with great agility from tree to tree.

MALAYAN FLYING LEMURS are usually found in rainforests but may also be found living on rubber plantations. They are about 1 foot in length and weigh between 2 and 3 pounds. They live in the trees and use large gliding membranes—which reach from their necks to their fingertips, toes, and tails—to travel distances of more than 200 feet. Webbed toes and folds of skin attached to their limbs also help them glide these distances. They feed upon leaves, shoots, buds, flowers, and soft fruits. They are found in Borneo, Java, Thailand, southern Indochina, Malaya, Sumatra, and adjacent islands.

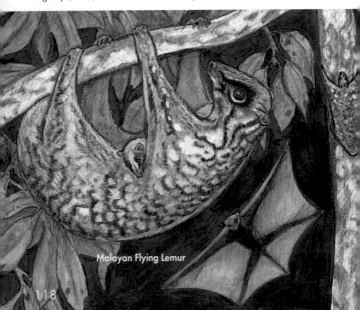

Malayan Flying Lemur

Bats

Unlike gliding mammals, bats are capable of true flight. They are also the most common rainforest mammals. (Worldwide, they are second in number of mammal species only to rodents.) Though many tropical species eat insects, others feed on nectar, pollen, seeds, and fruit. Most bats rely on sonarlike echolocation to find food. Fruit bats and flying foxes also have good vision. Some tropical bats pollinate flowers; others disperse seeds. In this way, bats help the rainforest replenish itself. But bats worldwide are now endangered, due to the extermination efforts of people and loss of habitat.

HONDURAN WHITE BATS are fruit bats less than 2 inches long found in Central America. They roost inside large, curled-up rainforest leaves and form a tent by cutting holes in the leaf. These spear-nosed bats are one of about 150 New World species. Most are gray, brown, or black. Only a few make tents.

Honduran White Bats

Fishing Bat

FISHING BATS, such as *Noctilio leporinus,* swoop down at night and skim large, open areas of water, catching fish with their clawed back feet. These large tropical American bats, with 2-foot wingspans, have bulldoglike faces—thus their nickname of bulldog bats. They roost in hollow trees and use echolocation to detect ripples on the water made by small fish. The bat eats the fish while hanging upside down on a branch.

INDIAN FLYING FOXES belong to a group of about 170 species known as Old World fruit bats, ranging from Africa to east Asia, Australia, and islands in the Pacific and Indian oceans. About 16 inches long and with wingspans of more than 4 feet, Indian Flying Foxes are the largest bats known. Found in Indonesia, their name comes from the foxlike shape of their heads. The fur on the head is reddish, though the muzzle is dark. The rest of the body is brownish black with yellow markings on the neck. Indian Flying Foxes feed at night on flowers, nectar, pollen, and fruit and maintain the same tree roosts throughout the year.

Indian Flying Foxes

COMMON VAMPIRE BATS are popularly believed to feed on human blood. And this species does feed on blood, though usually that of cattle or other domestic stock. Common Vampire Bats, about 3 to 4 inches long, forage at night, using razor-sharp teeth to slit the skin of prey. Grooves in their tongue serve as a kind of drinking straw, and the bats' saliva contains anticoagulants that prevent the wound from clotting. When feeding, a bat may consume up to 40 percent of its body weight in blood. Vampire bats are found mostly in Central and South Americas. Their bites can cause serious infections.

JAMAICAN FRUIT BATS have wingspans of more than a foot and dark brown coats. They are found from Mexico south to Brazil, where they will pluck fruits directly from the branches of large trees while flying. With their powerful chests and jaw muscles, they can carry heavy fruit more than 200 yards to their nests. Although fruit is their primary food, Jamaican Fruit Bats also feed on insects and flowers and pollinate many important tropical plants, such as the flowers of the Kapok Tree. They roost in caves, foliage, and hollow trees during the day.

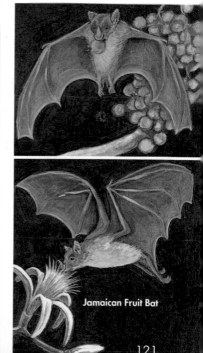

Jamaican Fruit Bat

Common Vampire Bat

121

Primates

Primates are the order of animal to which *Homo sapiens*—human beings—belong. They include our closest relatives in the animal kingdom, such as the great apes. The most notable features of mammals in this order are their highly developed brains and eyes and hands adopted for grasping.

Primates play an important role in the dispersal of tropical seeds. Many primates range far in search of food, in small groups or troops, and can cover many miles a day. Monkeys scatter seeds either by ingesting and later voiding them elsewhere or by dropping them to the forest floor while eating. Because of their large body size, relatively small troop size, and feeding behavior, wild primates are often severely affected by loss of habitat and hunting by humans.

Slow Loris

SLOW LORISES are tree-dwelling primates found in Indonesia. Their thick, tawny coats can be readily identified by the black stripe on their backs. Slow Lorises have short tails, usually concealed by the animals' long fur, and round faces with huge eyes for nocturnal vision. They live a mostly nocturnal existence, eating fruits and insects. These approximately foot-long primates are close relatives of bush babies and pottos. They move and climb very slowly. When frightened, they assume a frozen stance that can last for hours and help conceal them in the thick foliage of the rainforest.

BLACK LEMURS have very long fur, ranging from black in the males of the species to red in the females. The body is about 1 to 1½ feet in length, with the tail slightly longer. Like most lemurs, Black Lemurs are found only on the island of Madagascar. They live in the trees, usually in groups of about a dozen individuals, and eat leaves and fruits. Most active in the daytime, their strong hind legs are adapted for distance jumping.

Black Lemur

AYE-AYES (pronounced "eye-eyes") are distant relatives of lemurs. They are also among the rarest of mammals. These rodentlike primates are found solely in Madagascar, where they live in trees or amid patches of thick vegetation. Aye-ayes typically eat fruit and insect larvae—using a long middle finger to probe the fruit for the larvae—but they are especially fond of coconut meat and have teeth that can cut through the coconut's hard shell. Aye-ayes have large eyes, excellent night vision, blackish brown fur, and a body less than 2 feet in length. The tail is very squirrel-like—thick and bushy.

Aye-Aye

123

SPECTRAL TARSIERS are nocturnal animals native to Indonesia. They are found in the forests of Sulawesi, Great Sangihe, and Peleng. Their coats are gray, and their tails, with bushy tufts on the ends, are covered with scaley skin. Spectral Tarsiers live in family groups in the lower levels of the rainforest. They are monogamous and have a life span of about ten years, feeding on insects and other animals. Due to loss of habitat, they are now endangered.

Spectral Tarsier

Golden Lion Tamarins

GOLDEN LION TAMARINS get their name from their thick leonine manes of golden fur. A little less than 2 feet long with 1-foot-long tails, these endangered mammals live in remnant patches of the rainforest canopy, mostly along the Brazilian coastline. They eat both vegetation (mostly fruits and berries) and insects but will also eat lizards or even small birds on occasion.

BLACK HOWLER MONKEYS are primarily fruit-eating mammals about 2 feet long. They will also eat foliage. Males, which are much larger than females, have an all-black coat, females an olive-buff one. Found throughout much of South America, particularly southern Brazil and eastern Bolivia, Black Howlers live high in the canopy and come down to the understory mostly to feed. They are active in the daytime and often travel in groups of 4 to about 20 individuals, including babies.

Black Howler Monkey

White-faced Capuchin Monkey

WHITE-FACED CAPUCHIN MONKEYS are found in wet and dry forests as well as swamps and mangroves. They stay mainly in the rainforest's understory and mid-canopy but will often come to the ground to forage and play. They live in groups of 10 to 24 and feed on ripened or unripe fruits, cultivated crops, plants, snails and spiders, and nestling birds. Found from Belize south to northern and western Colombia, they are about 3 feet long, excluding the tail.

SPIDER MONKEYS have coats of short fur that come in a variety of shades, from yellowish gray, red, and golden brown to dark brown. The four known species of spider monkeys get their name from their slender body profiles and legs and their quick movements through the forest in a hand-over-hand manner along the underside of tree branches. Fruit eaters, they live in groups of about 20 individuals and are found mainly in the middle to upper canopy levels of Mexican and Central American rainforests.

Spider Monkeys

WOOLLY SPIDER MONKEYS, with thick, dense fur like that of woolly monkeys, are found mostly in south-eastern Brazil. About 1 to 1½ feet long, these monkeys are the largest and most apelike of the New World monkeys, foraging during the day for fruits, shoots, and buds. They live in troops of 25 or more members, led by a dominant male. Due to their low reproductive rate (mothers bear only one young each year) and hunting by humans, Woolly Spider Monkeys are now endangered.

Woolly Spider Monkey

PROBOSCIS MONKEYS are found in Borneo, where they inhabit river-banks and eat leaves. They can be instantly identified by their long noses, from which they get their name. In the males of the species, the nose often extends down over the mouth. Infants have bright blue facial skin. Full-grown monkeys are between 2 and 3 feet in length, with slightly shorter tails. Their coats are brown or pale red, and their long arms are adapted for swinging from tree branches. Although their chief habitat is lowland rainforest, these endangered monkeys are excellent swimmers and also live in riverine mangroves.

Proboscis Monkey

SIAMANGS are gibbons that live high up in the rainforest canopies of Southeast Asia and eat mainly ripe fruit and young leaves and, occasionally, small invertebrates. Almost 3 feet tall, the Siamang has a large throat sac that can be used to lengthen the distance that its loud screaming or barking calls can be heard. All nine species of gibbons, which are collectively known as the lesser apes, have an erect posture and wide swinging arms that allow them to move among and hang from branches in a unique way. Gibbons are monogamous, mating for life, and are highly territorial.

Siamangs

127

COMMON CHIMPANZEES inhabit the humid rainforests of western and central Africa. About 3 feet tall, they feed mainly on fruits, leaves, seeds, flowers, pith, resin, and bark, sampling from at least 20 different species of plants daily and more than 300 a year. Sometimes hard fruits and nuts are smashed open with a rock. Chimps will also eat ants, insect larvae, birds, pigs, antelopes—even juvenile monkeys. To capture stinging ants, they will stick a branch into a nest and let the ants crawl up it. In times of scarcity, they may forage in the nearby savanna. Like all great apes, they sleep in trees, in leafy beds made fresh nightly. Adults generally sleep alone.

Common Chimpanzees

ORANGUTANS are found in Borneo and Sumatra. They stay mostly in the trees, coming down to the forest floor only to gather branches for nests or food. About 4 feet tall and tailless, they have long, reddish fur. Males are about twice the size of females and have cheek flaps that enlarge during aggressive displays. Besides fruits (especially figs, jackfruits, lychees, durians, and mangoes) they eat leaves and shoots, insects, eggs, and small vertebrates such as birds and squirrels plus mineral-rich soil. The Orangutan's powerful jaws can chew through branches, tree bark, and spiny or thick-coated fruits. By watching hornbills, which eat the same fruit, they often learn the location of fruiting trees. Unlike most apes, adult Orangutans travel alone.

Orangutan

GORILLAS are the largest primates, belonging to the Pongidae family, or great apes, which also includes the Orangutans and chimpanzees. The male gorilla is much larger than the female. At 6 feet tall, he has an armspan of 9 to 10 feet.

Despite their appearance and reputation, gorillas are actually very gentle and rather shy. (Adult males may show aggression when guarding a family group or defending breeding rights.) Eating the leaves and stems of various herbs, shrubs, and vines found mostly on the forest floor, very stable family groups from about five to several dozen individuals live and forage in a small area, though they do not stay in one spot long enough to exhaust the food supply. Two of three subspecies live in the eastern and western lowland tropical rainforests in Nigeria, Cameroon, Zaire, and other equatorial African countries. The third, the Mountain Gorilla, lives on extinct volcanoes along the borders of Zaire, Rwanda, and Uganda.

Gorillas

129

Sloths and Anteaters

Sloths and anteaters are American mammals belonging to the rather primitive order Xenarthra. Sloths have thick hair, move slowly, and eat plants. Anteaters have long snouts for probing ant nests, sticky tongues for gathering insect prey, and no teeth in the front of their jaws.

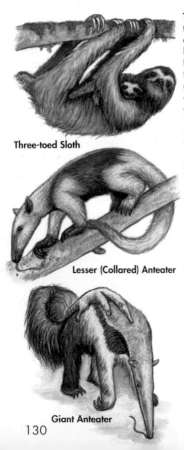

Three-toed Sloth

Lesser (Collared) Anteater

Giant Anteater

THREE-TOED SLOTHS live almost all their lives in trees, hanging upside down and holding on with powerful hooklike claws that are also used for defense. Found from Honduras to eastern Brazil to northern Argentina, sloths are among the slowest creatures on Earth, though they can speed up when pressed. About 2 feet long, they eat young leaves, soft twigs, and buds, especially those of the Cecropia Tree.

LESSER (COLLARED) ANTEATERS, or Tamanduas, are found from Mexico to Venezuela, northern Argentina, and southern Brazil. They have long, prehensile tails and live in the trees, where they gather up wood-eating insects such as termites. Although rather monkeylike, they have the long snouts and small eyes typical of anteaters. Their 2-foot-long bodies are covered by thick yellowish or brown coats.

GIANT ANTEATERS are found in both grasslands and tropical rainforests from the southern end of Mexico to Paraguay and northern Argentina. Almost 4 feet long excluding the tail, they feed only on large, ground-dwelling insects such as carpenter ants, using their long, powerful claws to open ant nests.

Rodents

Rodents are the largest order of mammals, though rainforests, have fewer than average. Most species, including rats and squirrels, are small and have sharp-edged incisor teeth used for gnawing. Rainforest rodents eat fruits and disperse seeds, especially those of understory plants such as palms. Their caches, often forgotten about, can develop into new plants.

CAPYBARAS are the largest living rodents. Their scientific name means "water pig," though they are neither pigs nor truly aquatic. Yet they often live near water, and their webbed feet help them escape into it. Found in South America, in groups of 40 or so members, mainly seagrass eaters, Capybaras are about 4 feet long and weigh 140 pounds. They are tailless, and their front legs are short. Their young are preyed on by vultures, caimans, and foxes. Adults are sometimes attacked by jaguars.

AGOUTIS are Central and South American relatives of that familiar childhood pet, the guinea pig. They have slender bodies, 1 to 2 feet in length; short tails; and long hind legs adapted for running. Their fur is short and brownish or orange in color. They eat the seeds and fruits of various rainforest trees, including palms, and disperse the seeds in the forest.

Agouti

Capybaras

Carnivores

All carnivores have claws and prominent canine teeth. Generally large and aggressive, carnivores feed mostly on flesh. Populations are widely scattered, with individual home ranges marked with scents. Huge tracts of land plus healthy food chains are needed for the survival of these mammals. Because of hunting by people and loss of habitat, their numbers have dwindled greatly, especially in rainforests. Carnivores include cats, dogs, bears, hyenas, and weasels, as well as civets, mongooses, and skunks.

OCELOTS are skillful climbers and are often found in the top parts of the rainforest canopy, hunting for birds and lizards. Their bodies grow to about 3 feet long, and their fur, usually yellowish or orange with a white underbelly, has black stripes or spots. Ocelots are one of 28 species of "small cats." Unlike the "big cats," such as Tigers and Jaguars, Ocelots feed in a crouched position rather than lying down and tuck their forepaws under their bodies when at rest. Good swimmers, they will also eat fish or small mammals when larger game is scarce. Found from North America to Argentina, Ocelots are endangered today.

Ocelot

Tiger

TIGERS are the largest of the cats, easily identified by their well-known fur—dark stripes alternating with reddish orange or yellow stripes. Like all big carnivores, tigers need large ranges to hunt for their food, about 30 square miles for males, 8 square miles for females. Tigers carefully patrol their home ranges, with males spraying the borders of their territory with a mixture of urine and anal gland secretions. Although capable of mounting a ferocious attack on their prey—usually deer or boar—these mammals are generally shy and rarely attack humans. Body length may be as great as 9 feet, with a 2- or 3-foot tail. Found in Southeast Asian rainforests and a few other places such as India and Siberia, Tigers today are everywhere extremely endangered.

133

LEOPARDS are found in many habitats, including African, Asian, and Indonesian rainforests. They grow to about 6 feet long, with a 4-foot tail. Though known for their tawny fur and black spots, some (known as Panthers) are all black. Leopards will prey on many species, including fish, snakes, birds, and domestic cattle. Like most large carnivores, they help regulate animal populations near the top of the food chain. Tigers stalk their prey; leopards hide in trees and ambush theirs. But like tigers, leopards are now endangered.

Leopard

Jaguar

JAGUARS are considered to be the New World equivalent of leopards. Living in very dense rainforest or swampy areas, usually somewhere near the water, they are excellent swimmers and eat a varied diet of deer, monkeys, rodents, and other mammals plus birds, fish, turtles, and frogs. Jaguars are solitary, and their home ranges can vary from 2 to 200 square miles, depending on the availability of prey. The Jaguar's 4- to 6-foot-long body is very compact, and its broad, massive head and extremely powerful paws make it a fierce predator. The range of this big cat is especially large, extending from the southwestern United States to central Argentina.

PUMAS go by many popular names, including Mountain Lion and Cougar, and are found from Canada to South America. In addition to the rainforest, Pumas can be found in mountain, swamp, and grassland environments. Their bodies are generally 3 to 5 feet in length, with 2- or 3-foot-long tails. They prey on deer, rodents, and cattle and hunt mostly at dawn and at sunset. Pumas are more adaptable than most big cats in terms of their range size. A large, stable prey population will result in their remaining in a rather small area for a long time, but they can alter their range seasonally, if they must, to find suitable prey.

Kinkajou

Puma

KINKAJOUS have short brown fur, bodies of $1\frac{1}{2}$ to 2 feet long, short legs, and prehensile tails. Found from southern Mexico to Brazil and usually classified as carnivores, these nocturnal mammals feed mostly on fruits and have long tongues that can reach deep into flowers to obtain nectar.

135

SUN BEARS, which live in Southeast Asia, are the smallest members of the bear family, growing to lengths of about 4 feet and often weighing less than 150 pounds. The female is slightly smaller than the male. The Sun Bear's coat is a dark brown or black color, but there may be white or orange markings on the chest, and the muzzle is light-colored. Short fur helps the animal keep cool in its equatorial habitat, where it feeds at night and sleeps during the day, climbing trees to find fruits, termites, birds, and small mammals.

SPECTACLED BEARS are the only bears from South America. Their fur is black or dark brown, with white markings around the eyes that look like spectacles. Spectacled Bears will sometimes emerge from the rainforest to hunt on the open plain. Although they occasionally prey on deer and other animals, they are primarily vegetarian and nest in trees either singly or with members of their immediate family.

Sun Bear

Spectacled Bear

Manatees

Manatees are marine mammals. The West Indian Manatee lives in coastal waters and rivers from North America to Brazil. Manatees grow up to 12 feet long and typically weigh between 500 and 1,200 pounds. Individuals may live 30 years or more. Often found floating just beneath the surface of the water—and therefore the victims of many motorboat collisions—members of this endangered species feed on aquatic vegetation. Females produce only one calf every two years or so.

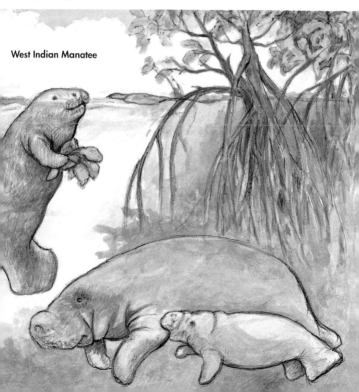

West Indian Manatee

Elephants

Elephants are the largest land animals and form their own order, Proboscidea. There are only two species, Asian and African. The most distinctive feature of elephants are their elongated trunks—extensions of the nose and upper lip—at the end of which are fingerlike extensors that can be used to pick up objects. Their ears are large, floppy, and fanlike. In most individuals the upper incisors extend from the mouth to form tusks. Elephants eat leaves, bark, shoots, fruits, and the roots of trees.

ASIAN ELEPHANTS are smaller than the African species, with a maximum weight of 11,000 to 12,000 pounds and heights of up to about 10 feet. The back is humped and the trunk relatively rigid, with only a single flexible extensor at the end. Some females lack tusks. There are four distinct subspecies: the Indian, the Ceylon, the Sumatran, and the Malaysian. Although all the various subspecies have patchy distribution today and are in danger of extinction, Asian elephants were once found in a wide variety of habitats, including tropical rainforests.

Asian Elephant

AFRICAN ELEPHANTS are nearly 1½ times as large, on average, as Asian elephants. The male will commonly weigh in at 14,000 pounds, though a few individuals may grow to much greater sizes. Heights of over 12 feet have been reported. The African species is identified not only by its greater size but by its more flexible trunk, which has at its tip two extensors, and the downward curve of its huge back. The Forest Elephant subspecies is smaller, on average, than the Savanna and has bigger ears. As the name implies, the Forest Elephant is found in the rainforest, but it often interbreeds with the Savanna. Hybrids of the two can be found both in the forest and on the open plains.

African Elephant

Odd-toed Hoofed Mammals

As their name implies, these hoofed mammals (including horses, tapirs, rhinoceroses, and zebras), which once roamed across the open plains, have an odd number of toes, the middlemost of which is very long. Though they eat mostly plants, they will also eat insects, other arthropods, and small vertebrates. Earlier members of this group helped cultivate the rainforests by dispersing huge amounts of fruits and seeds.

Brazilian Tapir

BRAZILIAN TAPIRS are found in much of Central and South Americas, particularly Brazil. The small head of this tapir, with its elephant-like snout that curves downward, sits atop a tailless 6-foot-long body. With short legs and brown or yellow fur, these tapirs are largely nocturnal and often live in swampy areas or near rivers; they eat water plants and grasses plus the leaves, buds, fruits, and young twigs of shrubs.

Malayan Tapir

MALAYAN TAPIRS are found in the dense rainforests of Indonesia and Burma. At night they feed in forest clearings and riverbanks, eating fruits and browsing on low branches and grasses. They travel along as they feed, eating only small amounts of vegetation before moving on. Good swimmers, they spend a lot of time in the water. Malayan Tapirs grow to nearly 8 feet in length and live about 30 years. Tailless, their bodies are mostly black, with white in the middle. Habitat loss and overhunting has left them endangered.

INDIAN RHINOCEROSES inhabit northern India. Their thick, gray, armorlike skin is gathered at the head to form a powerful horn. Like most rhinos, they prefer to live in swampy areas, spending most of their time in water and eating plants, especially leaves and soft shoots. They grow to lengths of more than 12 feet, with 2-foot-long tails and 18-inch horns. On land they are capable of speeds of up to 40 miles per hour. All male rhinos are capable of fighting and inflicting severe wounds with their front horns. Rhinos are in danger partly because, in northern India and the Far East, these horns plus the rhinos' hooves, blood, and urine are thought to be an aphrodisiac and have other "medicinal" powers.

Sumatran Rhinoceros

SUMATRAN RHINOCEROS, which lives in mountainous rainforests of ndonesia is the world's smallest at about $\frac{1}{3}$ the weight of the Indian Rhino.

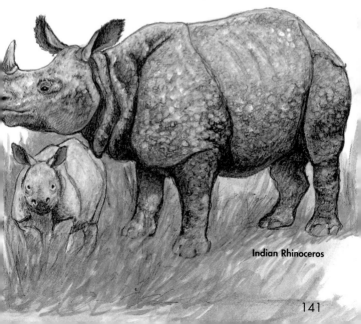

Indian Rhinoceros

141

Even-toed Hoofed Mammals

Sometimes referred to as ungulates, these mammals form one of the most varied orders and include cattle, antelopes, gazelles, camels, goats, sheep, deer, giraffes, and pigs. Members are distinguished by having an even number of toes. Not strictly rainforest dwellers, many of these browsing animals spend a lot of time in open grasslands, savannas, or deserts. Yet, as seasons change, some of these mammals also visit rainforests, usually traveling in groups or herds.

BARKING DEER, or Muntjacs, found in Southeast Asia, browse on many forest plants, and their bodies range from about 3 to 4 feet in length, with the male sporting a small pair of antlers. The species gets its name from the barking sound this solitary mammal makes when disturbed.

Barking Deer

Lesser Mouse Deer

LESSER MOUSE DEER are also found in parts of southeastern Asia. They are nocturnal and very shy, secretive creatures, feeding mainly on fallen fruit and some foliage. They are about 18 inches in length, excluding their tails.

GIANT FOREST HOGS inhabit the tropical rainforests of Africa, where they graze in evergreen clearings. They have dark brown, bristly coats and bodies from 5 to 8 feet in length. These hogs can communicate with family members, using a nearly continuous series of grunting sounds and squeaks. They are also carriers of African Swine Fever, which kills domestic pigs and is transmitted by ticks.

BLACK DUIKERS are antelopes that are found in western Africa. They grow to only about 3 feet in length and have dark brown or black fur on their backs. Their long hind legs are specially adapted for running and leaping. Altogether there are 17 species of duikers, all in Africa. Their name, which is derived from the Afrikaans word for diver, refers to their habit of diving into forest foliage to avoid being seen. Duikers are solitary rather than gregarious creatures, with pairs mating for life. Black Duikers come out to feed only at night. They prefer leaves, shoots, fruits, seeds, and bark but will also eat insects, carrion, and small birds.

Giant Forest Hogs

Maxwell's Duiker

Black Duiker

MAXWELL'S DUIKERS have coats that range in color from blue-gray to grayish brown. The males of all the subspecies have horns, but many of the females do not. Maxwell's Duikers grow to a little over 3 feet in length and weigh about 20 pounds.

COLLARED PECCARIES, which are related to domestic pigs, are found along the edges of Central and South American rainforests. They are 2 to 3 feet long, with short tails. Their coats are dark brown, with white markings at the neck. Much of their diet consists of fruits and grasses, and their sharp tusks are used to cut roots, a favorite food. They will also attack and eat poisonous snakes. Herds of a dozen to 50 animals will subdivide into family groups. Territories are marked by a scent secreted from a rump gland, and dung pile "markers" within the peccary's territory often contain large amounts of undigested seeds that later germinate.

Collared Peccaries

Okapi

OKAPIS are found in western Africa. Relatives of the giraffe, they have dark brown heads and bodies (excluding their tails) about 6 to 7 feet long, but the black and white stripes on their legs resemble those of a zebra. These shy, nocturnal creatures are difficult to spot, since they run away at the first sound of an intruder. They eat mostly leaves and fruits, using their long, highly developed tongues to procure food. The male has a pair of short horns.

144

THE FUTURE OF THE RAINFORESTS

PEOPLE AND TROPICAL RAINFORESTS have been closely linked for many thousands of years. From archaeological, historical, and even ecological evidence it is clear that rainforests have long supported rich and diverse cultures of native peoples, cultures now being lost along with rainforest plants, animals, and ecosystems. These cultures managed to use the forests as vital resources without destroying them. Learning how they did this may help us to better protect these forests now and in the future.

Subsistence farming was the main agricultural practice of many ancient native cultures. Subsistence farmers raised food crops mainly for their families and neighbors.

In Central American rainforests, for example, the Maya developed small, highly diversified garden plots of various food crops such as corn (maize), beans, and squash. They sold or traded little of what they harvested. Used plots were allowed to remain fallow for years, which let the jungle vegetation reestablish itself. Trees and plants were cut down to provide building materials, tools, and medicines. The forests also offered the Maya a sense of spirituality.

Mayan society, with its sophisticated culture and successful system of agriculture, flourished for more than 600 years in the rainforests. The same agricultural methods are still practiced in some rainforest regions today.

Another ancient technique developed by the indigenous peoples of the rainforest was the slash-and-burn method of clearing plots of land to create farms. The cut vegetation was left to dry wherever it fell. It was later burned, with the ash serving as a temporary fertilizer. When the land again became infertile, the farmers would move on and clear new sections of forest. Slash-and-burn is still practiced today but on a much larger scale, resulting in the destruction of large areas of rainforest.

Central Africa: A **Mbuti** family cooking food.

Borneo: A **Penan** man using a blowgun to hunt game.

Amazon: Yanomami Indians with harvest of plantains.

Some native peoples in the rainforest concentrated on hunting meat and gathering up wild plants as food rather than farming. The Mbuti Pygmies of central Africa and the Agta people of the Philippines today still hunt with spears, blowguns, and bows and arrows or use traps and nets to catch their prey. A few native rainforest peoples fish.

The hunting of large animals by humans has been a part of rainforest life for centuries. New World rainforest natives have hunted monkeys, peccaries, deer, armadillos, and large rodents. Intensely hunted rainforest birds include curassows, toucans, and macaws. However, modern-day large-scale commercial hunting and the capture of animals for export have added hugely to the losses of large rainforest animals and damaged the whole rainforest ecology.

Familiar vegetables such as tomatoes, eggplants, sweet potatoes, cucumbers, pumpkins, squashes, and watermelons were first cultivated from wild forms in native Latin American tropical rainforests thousands of years ago. Cacao (cocoa beans), bananas, and spices are grown today in many regions. Chocolate is made from the fruit that grows on the Cacao Tree. Cacao was once farmed in small plots by the Maya and other Indians in Central America and Mexico. The Maya drank a crude pastelike beverage of chocolate mixed with cornmeal, vanilla, and chile peppers for some rituals and ceremonies. The arrival of the Spanish in the New World led to an expansion of cacao farming. Cacao is now grown in many Asian and African rainforests, mainly for exportation.

Today bananas are grown chiefly by large corporations that export huge numbers to North America and Europe. Spices such as black pepper, mace, nutmeg, cinnamon, and allspice plus flavorings such as vanilla all come from trees or plants that grow in tropical rainforests. Vanilla comes from the world's largest orchid plant. Nutmeg and mace come from the fruit of the nutmeg tree.

(Left) Fruit and flower on a **banana tree**, (middle) **Cacao pods** on tree, (right) **Coffee berries** contain the beans (seeds).

A French scientist exploring the Amazon in the eighteenth century observed native people using a white substance called latex that was obtained by cutting into a rainforest tree and "bleeding" it. The Indians used hardened latex, known for its great elasticity, to make many things. The scientist brought the latex back to Europe, where it was eventually used to "rub" out pencil marks, giving it the name "rubber." Although synthetic rubber, developed near the beginning of World War II, is generally used in place of real rubber today, natural rubber is still used for making certain delicate items such as surgical gloves and condoms.

MODERN CIVILIZATION has spread to many tropical rain-forest regions that were once inhabited only by native peoples. Although this incursion began several centuries ago, it was not until the 1950s that large-scale movements of outsiders into tropical rainforests began resulting in the rapid and widespread destruction of those forests. Small-scale farming in the forests gave way, in large part, to a plantation-style agriculture designed to produce cash crops for export rather than to feed local populations. Because the damage to tropical rainforests is so widespread, it is probably permanent.

Cleared areas, once spent of their soil nutrients, are no longer allowed to lie fallow but are converted into cattle pastures. Cattle grazing, especially in the Amazon regions of South America, alters the natural distribution of soil and litter nutrients such as nitrogen, potassium, and calcium. This in turn lowers the chances of the natural forest recolonizing the area. Persistent heavy rains and the constant pounding of hooves erode the thin soil. Hardy, exotic

Central America: Rainforest destroyed for grazing cattle.

species of grass are grown to feed beef cattle in regions once covered with forest. The grasses then choke off the native plant species before they can reestablish themselves. Eventually these regions will be barren and thus totally useless for any kind of agriculture or ranching.

By some estimates, 50 to 150 species of plants and animals become extinct each day as the rainforests are cleared. About 50 million acres of tropical rainforest are now lost every year, or approximately 5,800 acres every hour. If destruction continues at the current rate, one-fourth of all the species on Earth today will be extinct by the year 2050. The rainforests themselves will vanish in less than 200 years.

Madagascar: Clearing of the rainforests for timber causes erosion and destruction of the land.

RESCUING THE RAINFORESTS is a task requiring the participation of government and private enterprise, educators, conservationists, and scientists. Rainforests are home to vast biological resources. As the rainforests continue to vanish, these resources will vanish with them.

Tropical rainforests are often viewed as hostile environments. Some outsiders have contracted severe tropical diseases such as malaria, yellow fever, and African sleeping sickness. Such illnesses seem to be much less of a problem for the native peoples of rainforests, and only a few species cause or transmit the known harmful diseases. On the other hand, tropical rainforests are vast chemical libraries with a wide variety of substances employed by living things for defense or communication. Many of these substances are now or could possibly be used in the future for treating such devastating illnesses as cancer, heart disease, and AIDS.

Saving the rainforests is the responsibility of each individual country, but many rainforest nations are very poor. More affluent governments around the world and the international banking community must help out. Reducing debt in return for setting aside protected tracts of land has helped slow the destruction of some rainforests. Costa Rica and several other nations have developed extensive park systems to attract scientists and nature lovers. This so-called ecotourism has become a major source of income in some rainforest areas. Financial support must continue to flow into the tropics, as well as technical assistance. Rescuing the rainforests also means fewer people moving into rainforest regions. Tropical countries are quickly running out of room to accommodate their bulging, still-hungry populations.

Tropical rainforests can be valuable resources for things other than farmland and timber. For that reason they must be preserved, rather than destroyed. Tropical rainforests are also beautiful, unique environments that deserve to be protected simply because they exist.

TROPICAL RAINFOREST SPECIES LIST: COMMON AND SCIENTIFIC NAMES

The alphabetical listing below gives the common names of most of the species depicted in this book, followed by their scientific names (genus and species) in *italics*. The numbers refer to the text pages on which that entry can be found. An asterisk (*) shows that various related species are grouped together here under the genus or family name.

68	Acacia ant (*Pseudomyrmex*)	**60**	Blue Morpho (*Morpho peleides*)
105	Acorn Woodpecker (*Melanerpes formicivorus*)	**63**	Blue Butterfly (*Lycaenidae**)
139	African Elephant (*Loxodonta africana*)	**78**	Boa Constrictor (*Boa constrictor constrictor*)
131	Agouti (*Dasyprocta**)	**140**	Brazilian Tapir (*Tapirus terrestris*)
68	Army Ant (*Eciton burchelli*)	**55**	Bush Katydid (*Orophus conspersus*)
138	Asian Elephant (*Elephas maximus*)	**82**	Bushmaster (*Lachesis muta*)
123	Aye-aye (*Daubentonia madagascariensis*)	**111**	Canada Warbler (*Wilsonia canadensis*)
67	Azteca Ant (*Azteca**)	**131**	Capybara (*Hydrochaerus hydrochaeris*)
110	Bare-necked Umbrellabird (*Cephalopterus glabricollis*)	**70**	Carpenter Bee (*Xylocopa fimbriata*)
142	Barking Deer (*Muntiacus muntjak*)	**94**	Cattle Egret (*Bubulcus ibis*)
95	Barred Forest Falcon (*Micrastur ruficollis*)	**51**	Cecropia Tree (*Cecropia peltela*)
37	Bengal Clock Vine (*Thunbergia grandiflora*)	**61**	Clearwing Satyr (*Haetera macleannania*)
44	Bird-of-paradise Plant (*Heliconia**)	**144**	Collared Peccary (*Tayassu tajacu*)
125	Black Howler Monkey (*Alouatta palliata*)	**128**	Common Chimpanzee (*Pan troglodytes*)
123	Black Lemur (*Lemur macaco*)	**84**	Common Iguana (*Iguana iguana*)
100	Black Rail (*Laterallus jamaicensis*)	**86**	Common Tegu (*Tupinambis teguixin*)
97	Black Vulture (*Coragyps atratus*)	**121**	Common Vampire Bat (*Desmodus rotundus*)
143	Black-fronted Duiker (*Cephalophorus niger*)	**99**	Congo Peacock (*Afropavo congensis*)

63 Copper Butterfly (Lycaenidae*)

82 Coral Snake (Micrurus nigrocinctus)

46 Cortes Tree (Tabebuia chrysantha)

96 Crested Caracara (Polyborus plancus)

50 Cycad Tree (Zamia skinneri)

39 Dancing Lady Orchid (Oncidium pusillum)

87 Double-crested Basilisk (Basiliscus plumifrons)

42 Dieffenbachia (Dieffenbachia*)

93 Double-wattled Cassowary (Casuarius casuarius)

57 Dung Beetle (Dichotamius carolinnus)

79 Emerald Tree Boa (Corallus caninus)

83 Estuarine Crocodile (Crocodylus porosus)

81 Eyelash Viper (Bothrops schlegeli)

80 Fer-de-lance (Bothrops atrox)

104 Fiery-billed Aracari (Pteroglossus frantzii)

35 Filmy Fern (Trichomanes krausii)

84 Flying Dragon (Draco volans)

81 Gaboon Viper (Bitis gobonica)

47 Gavilan Tree (Pentaclethra macroloba)

130 Giant Anteater (Myrmecophaga tridactyla)

72 Giant Damselfly (Magaloprepus coerulatus)

143 Giant Forest Hog (Hylochoerus meinertzhageni)

54 Giant Red-winged Grasshopper (Tropidacris cristata)

67 Giant Tropical Ant (Paraponera clavata)

88 Glass Frog (Centrolenella euknemos or fleischmanni)

124 Golden Lion Tamarin (Leontopithecus rosalia)

73 Golden Orb Weaver Spider (Nephila clavipes)

57 Golden Scarab Beetle (Plusiotus batesi)

90 Golden Toad (Bufo periglenes)

129 Gorilla (Gorilla gorilla)

100 Gray-necked Wood-rail (Aramides cajanea or Crax rubra?)

76 Green Turtle (Chelonia mydas)

64 Green Urania Moth (Urania fulgens)

85 Green Water Dragon (Physignathus concincus)

54 Green-and-gold Grasshopper (Drymophilacris bimaculata)

63 Hairstreak Butterfly (Lycaenidae*)

57 Harlequin Beetle (Acrocinus longimanus)

96 Harpy Eagle (Harpia harpyia)

117 Hispaniola Solenodon (Solenodon paradoxus)

120 Indian Flying Fox (Pteropus vampyrus)

141 Indian Rhinoceros (Rhinoceros unicornis)

63 Ithomiine Butterfly (Mechanitis isthmia)

134 Jaguar (Panthera onca)

121 Jamaican Fruit Bat (Artibeus jamaicensis)

45 Kapok Tree (Ceiba pentandra)

104 Keel-billed Toucan (Ramphastos sulfuratus)

97 King Vulture (Sarcoramphus papa)

135 Kinkajou (Potos flavus)

87 Komodo Dragon (Varanus komodoensis)

43 Lady Lips Plant (Cephaelis tomentosa)

FOR MORE INFORMATION

ORGANIZATIONS

Bat Conservation International, P.O. Box 162603, Austin, TX 78716 (512-327-9721)

Conservation International, 1015 18th Street, NW, Suite 1000, Washington, D.C. 20036 (202-429-5660)

RARE Center for Tropical Conservations, 1616 Walnut Street, Suite 911, Philadelphia, PA 19103 (215-735-3510)

Rainforest Action Network, 450 Sansome, Suite 700, San Francisco, CA 94111 (415-398-4404)

Rainforest Alliance, 65 Bleeker Street, New York, NY 10012 (212-677-1900)

The Nature Conservancy, 1815 North Lynn Street, Arlington, VA 22209 (703-841-5300)

World Wildlife Fund, 1250 24th Street, NW, Washington, D.C. 20037 (202-293-4800)

BOOKS

Allen, Paul H. *The Rain Forests of Golfo Dulce*. University of Florida Press, Gainesville, FL, 1956.

Bates, Henry W. *The Naturalist on the River Amazons* (reprint of original ed., 1864, John Murray, London). University of California Press, Berkeley and Los Angeles, 1962.

Belt, Thomas. *The Naturalist in Nicaragua* (reprint of original edition, 1874, John Murray, London). University of Chicago Press, Chicago, 1985.

Caufield, Catherine. *In the Rainforest*. A. A. Knopf, New York, 1985.

Forsyth, Adrian, and K. Miyata. *Tropical Nature: Life and Death in the Rain Forests of Central and South America*. Scribner's, New York, 1987.

Hogue, Charles L. *Latin American Insects and Entomology*. University of California Press, Berkeley and Los Angeles, 1993.

Janzen, Daniel H., ed. *Costa Rican Natural History*. University of Chicago Press, Chicago, 1983.

McDade, Lucinda A., K. S. Bawa, H. A. Hespenheide, and G. S. Hartshorn, eds. *La Selva: Ecology and Natural History of a Neotropical Rain Forest*. University of Chicago Press, Chicago, 1994.

Mitchell, Andrew W. *The Enchanted Canopy*. Macmillan, New York, 1986.

Perry, Don. *Life Above the Jungle Floor*. Simon & Schuster, New York, 1987.

Quintero, Diomedes, and A. Aiello. *Insects of Panama and Mesoamerica*. Oxford University Press, London, 1992.

Richards, Paul W. *The Tropical Rainforest: An Ecological Study*. Cambridge University Press, Cambridge, 1952.

Whitmore, Theodore C., and C. P. Burnham. *Tropical Rain Forests of the Far East*. Oxford University Press, London, 1975.

Wilson, Edmund O. *The Diversity of Life*. Belknap Press of Harvard University Press, Cambridge, MA, 1992.

INDEX

Note: *Italicized* numbers refer to illustrations.